Nelson's Victory

TRAFALGAR & TRAGEDY

Nelson's Victory

TRAFALGAR & TRAGEDY

KEVIN JACKSON

TSB & Leapfrog Press
London and New York

To Shan Lancaster

Nelson's Victory: Trafalgar & Tragedy
9 8 7 6 5 4 3 2 1

First published in the United Kingdom by TSB, 2021

TSB is an imprint of:
Can of Worms Enterprises Ltd
7 Peacock Yard, London SE17 3LH
www.canofworms.net

First published in the United States by Leapfrog Press, 2021
Leapfrog Press Inc.
P.O. Box 1293, Dunkirk, NY 14048
www.leapfrogpress.com

© 2020 Kevin Jackson
Author portrait: © Marzena Pogorzały
www.marzenapogorzaly.com

Cover, text and map design: James Shannon
Set in Adobe Garamond Pro and 1689 GLC Garamond Pro

ISBN: 978-1-911673-06-4 (UK paperback)
ISBN: 978-1-948585-19-4 (US paperback)

Printed and bound in the United Kingdom

British Library Cataloguing in Publication Data

A catalogue record for this book is available from the British Library

Kevin Jackson was an English writer, broadcaster and film-maker. He had also been a Teaching Fellow of Vanderbilt University, Nashville; a radio producer and television director for the BBC; Associate Arts Editor for *The Independent* and a roving reporter for *Night and Day* Magazine, where his assignments included a week on a fishing boat in Atlantic waters, a training mission on a Royal Navy aircraft carrier and a helicopter flight to an oil rig in the Caspian, near Baku. His books include *Constellation of Genius* (Hutchinson), a history of modernism which was a Book of the Week in *The Guardian* and a Book of the Year in the *Express*; *Invisible Forms* (Picador); *Carnal* (Pallas Athene); and the authorized biography *Humphrey Jennings* (Picador). He collaborated with the cartoonist Hunt Emerson on several projects, including *Bloke's Progress* (Ruskin Comics), a comic fable inspired by the writings of John Ruskin; a version of Dante's *Inferno* (Knockabout); and, most recently, *Lives of the Great Occultists* (Knockabout). His long narrative poem, *Greta and the Labrador* (Holland House Books) was charmingly illustrated by the artist Jo Dalton. Jackson's other regular collaborators included the cameraman Spike Geilinger, who shot most of his independent films, and the musician Colin Minchin, with whom he co-wrote the rock opera *Bite*. He was a Fellow of the Royal Society of Arts, a Companion of the Guild of St George, and a Regent of the Collège de 'Pataphysique. At his untimely death, Kevin Jackson had completed four of the titles in his Seven Ships Maritime History series. We hope to publish Captain Cook's *Endeavour* in due course. Though each volume tells an independent tale, the series also charts the rise and decline of Britain as the world's greatest naval power.

TSB | Can of Worms will proudly publish Kevin Jackson's wonderful homage to TE Lawrence: *Legion: Thirteen Ways of Looking at Lawrence of Arabia* in 2022. Many moving obituaries were published shortly after Kevin Jackson's death, and links can be found at: www.canofworms.net/KevinJackson.

Production and Publishing Credits

A considerable number of people are involved in realising an author's work as a finished book on the shelf of your local library, bookshop or online retailer. TSB would like to acknowledge the critical input of:

Cover design, layout and cartography. TSB/Can of Worms has benefitted from a longstanding relationship with James Shannon on book production and website development for many of its own titles as well as some of Can of Worms's consultancy clients. For this *Seven Ships Maritime History* Series, James has undertaken the cover design, page layout as well as map design. James and further examples of his work can be found at: www.jshannon.com

Editorial. Editorial has been provided by Tobias Steed, publisher of TSB/Can of Worms. Tobias's career in publishing has spanned forty plus years having started as an editorial assistant for Johns Hopkins University Press in Baltimore, co-founder of illustrated travel guides publishing company, Compass American Guides, Oakland, California, Associate Publisher and Director of New Media at Fodor's/Random House, New York, and most recently founder and publisher of Can of Worms Enterprises Ltd. www.canofworms.net

Ship Plans. Permission for the use of the ship plans in the *Seven Ships Maritime History* series* have been provided to TSB/Can of Worms by Vadiim Eidlin at Best Ship Models, a company that provides accurate ship plans designed especially for model shipbuilders. Their collection includes 500+ plans for beginners and professional modelers. www.bestshipmodels.com

*the plans used in *Darwin's Odyssey: The Voyage of the Beagle* are from Alamy.com

Sales and Marketing. Sales and Marketing for the Seven Ships Maritime History and all other Leapfrog Press titles in the US and Canada is overseen by Consortium Book Sales and Distribution (CBSD) St. Paul, Minnesota 55114 www.cbsd.com. Sales and Marketing for the Seven Ships Maritime History and all other TSB/Can of Worms titles is overseen by Garry Manning of The Manning Partnership. Established in 1997, The Manning Partnership provides a complete Sales, Marketing & Distribution solution for TSB/Can of Worms and other publishers to the UK and English language export markets. Garry also oversees the TSB/Can of Worms relationship with our distributor, GBS/Penguin Random House. www.manning-partnership.co.uk

Publicity. All publicity enquiries should be directed to Tobias Steed. info@canofworms.net. Further information and resources for the *Seven Ships Maritime History* series can be found at www.canofworms.net/seven-ships

Seven Ships Maritime History Series – a Note from the author

In the summer of 2006, about five years before the Syrian Civil War began, I spent a couple of weeks in Damascus. In theory I was doing some informal research about Lawrence of Arabia, but in reality I mostly wandered the streets and gazed at the buildings and was touched by the exquisite good manners of the local people. In the afternoons, when the heat became oppressive for a pale European, I went into the Umayyad Mosque – infidels are quite welcome there – and squatted next to one of the pillars, and read the book I had brought with me: a hardback edition of Livingstone Lowes' *The Road to Xanadu*, which is a wonderful exploration of all the travel narratives that fed the imagination of the young Coleridge. It was delicious to escape from the uncomfortable warmth of a Damascene summer and daydream about the snow and the icebergs and the dark, chill waters that the ancient mariners had met when they ventured to the far north.

The extracts from old diaries and letters and memoirs cited in this study re-awoke in me that sense of wonder which the best sailors' tales have always inspired, especially in children. When I put the book down to daydream, I began to think of how fascinating it would be for me to find out more about maritime history, and to tell the stories of the greatest British ships over the centuries of the Western maritime expansion. It was not hard to choose seven famous vessels for seven books, each of which would have its own major themes: *Golden Hind* (exploration, plunder), *Mayflower* (religion, emigration), *Endeavour* (science, colonialism), *Bounty* (rebellion, survival), *Victory* (war, heroism), *Beagle* (biology, genius) and *Endurance* (leadership, heroism, survival). Each volume would be self-contained, but would also mark a chapter in the rise and decline of British maritime power and the creation of the modern world.

The idea came to me whole, in a single dreamy afternoon, and I knew it was what I wanted to do next. Now all I had to do was write my tales: the stories of Seven Ships.

Kevin Jackson, 2020

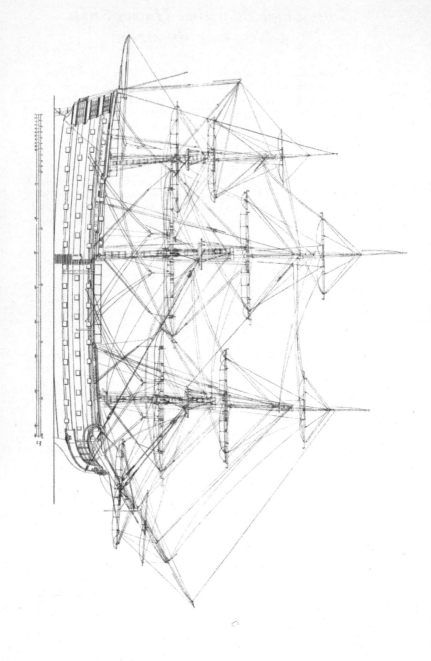

Table of Contents

Prelude: Nelson's *Victory*   11

Chapter One   Youth (1758 – 77)   21

Chapter Two   Early Navy Years (1778 – 86)   29

Chapter Three   England, Corsica, Cape St Vincent   49
                   – *England: Five Years of Rejection*
                   – *The Return*
                   – *January – August 1794:*
                       The Corsican Campaign
                   – *14 February 1797:*
                       The Battle of Cape St Vincent

Chapter Four   Egypt, Naples, Sicily, 1798 – 99   73
                   The Battle of the Nile
                   Naples and Sicily
                   Emma and William

Chapter Five   Copenhagen, England the   93
                   War with France
                   – *The Passage Home and the Battle of*
                       Copenhagen
                   – *The Battle of Copenhagen (1801)*
                   – *Merton and the Prelude to Trafalgar*
                   – *The Victory*

Chapter Six   Trafalgar and Afterwards   117

Prelude

Nelson's Victory

Trafalgar Day, 21 October 1805, Dawn to Noon

The morning dawned at about 5.30 AM. After some initial mist, soon burned off by the sun, the day was clear and would remain bright and warm for hours, with a light westerly wind. By mid-day the temperature had risen to 21° Celsius, roughly 70° Fahrenheit. More ominously, there was a swell that gradually mounted through the day: a major Atlantic storm was brewing. The two fleets preparing for deadly combat were deployed off the south-west coast of Spain – the British, about 22 miles from Cape Trafalgar; the French and Spanish allies, about 12 miles.

Lord Horatio Nelson, aboard his magnificent flagship *HMS Victory* – probably the finest vessel in the Royal Navy, and certainly the most handsome and powerful of the many ships he had captained – caught his first glimpse of the enemy fleet to the east as small silhouettes against the rising sun. Thirty-three ships of the line, with seven armed frigates and corvettes: a total of forty ships. The

English fleet was smaller: twenty-seven ships of the line with six frigates, a total of thirty-three. On the face of it, the English were dangerously outnumbered.

The nearest of the enemy ships were now about 10 miles away. Sailing at 3 knots, that distance would narrow at a rate of about one mile per hour – painfully slow. Nelson's adversary in the battle to come was a man he had faced and beaten before: Admiral Pierre Villeneuve, a survivor of Nelson's overwhelming victory at Aboukir Bay, near the Nile, in August 1798. Nelson's ferocious attack had all but wiped out the French squadron there: nine ships of the line captured and two destroyed; 1,700 men killed, 1,500 wounded and 2,000 taken prisoner. The French historian René Maine sums it up: "In a single night, Nelson ... had inflicted on the French navy the most bloody disaster in its history." Some historians consider Nelson's action on the Nile of greater strategic importance than any of his other triumphs.

Admiral Villeneuve had every reason to be anxious about the fighting ahead. It took about ten minutes after first light for him to be able to have a have a clear view of the British fleet, which, while numerically inferior, he knew to have more talented, professional officers, more disciplined and dedicated sailors, and better gunnery.

Temperamentally, and in almost every other respect, the two admirals could not have been more different. At the age of forty-seven, and with more than three decades of naval service behind him, Nelson had risen from almost complete obscurity to become the most famous, most revered and even the most loved of Englishmen. His talents were many: an almost supernatural ability to read men and actions; swiftness and certainty in decision-making; a capacity to train men, and to lead them. There was even a recognised term for his power to inspire: "the Nelson touch".

These virtues were in addition to his ruthless severity towards his enemies and a tactical brilliance that many thought (and still think) could only be summed up by the word *genius*. One aspect of that genius can be summed up in a single phrase: Nelson was a rule-breaker. Again and again, he ignored long-standing conventions of naval warfare, and in some cases defied his superiors' direct orders. Again and again, his instincts proved sound, steered him to victory, and won the enthusiastic applause of men who might otherwise have had him court-martialled and imprisoned.

At a time when the English were terrified by the prospect of imminent invasion by Napoleon's armies – and they were right to be frightened, because Napoleon had not merely plotted invasion but prepared for it at colossal expense – Nelson was a national hero. To his most ardent admirers, he was, indeed a saviour, and the terms in which he was lauded by them often echoed those traditionally used to praise Jesus Christ.

Villeneuve, just five years younger than Nelson, was no competition. To be sure, he was not without his virtues. Even though Napoleon screamed that Villeneuve was a coward, he was, in fact, a fairly sound fighter, an honourable man both in public and private matters, and in his own quiet way a patriot. But his nature was sceptical and vacillating. He was distant from his men, overwhelmed by the tempestuous rages and brutal manners of his commander-in-chief Napoleon, altogether lacking in the imagination, verve and originality that made Nelson such a deadly foe. Defeatist, and at times actually despairing, he could hardly have been a worse person to command an attack against the Victor of the Nile.

As soon as visibility was good enough, Nelson had his signal hoisted, forming the order to sail against the enemy in two columns: "Set course east-north-east." Villeneuve saw that the two columns of Nelson's force were sailing directly at his line, aiming at the centre and the rear. Nelson's strategy would have been plain to the Frenchman. By throwing most of his force against these sections, surrounding those vessels to the south, Nelson could inflict massive damage without giving the Combined Fleet time to turn and come to their aid.

There was an obvious move Villeneuve might have made: order his van to wear round and double on the rear squadron, so as to surround the British as they attacked. Some of Villeneuve's captains watched eagerly for the signal to do just this. But no signal came.

Immediately after giving his signals, Nelson went downstairs to his cabin and wrote a note to the woman he loved more than anyone in the world: his mistress, Emma Hamilton. They had first met as early as 1790, on his first trip to Naples. Both of them were married at the time – Horatio to the rather prim and bloodless "Fanny", Emma to the much older Sir William Hamilton, a distinguished diplomat and connoisseur whose interests ranged from the arts of classical Antiquity to vulcanology. Nelson and Hamilton became the best of friends, and the scholar seems to have been entirely complaisant when he discovered that the younger man had made him a cuckold. The affair with Emma soon became well-known throughout England. Opinion was divided between those who thought that a conquering hero deserved a beautiful consort, and those who found his conduct unworthy of a gentleman. But Nelson was entirely besotted with Emma, and unworried by the disapproval of respectable society. In his eyes, it was she and not Fanny who was his true wife and soulmate.

> My dearest beloved Emma, the dear friend
> of my bosom ... May the God of Battles
> crown my endeavours with success, at all
> events I will take care that my name shall
> ever be most near to you and Horatia
> [their illegitimate daughter, on whom he
> doted], both of whom I love as much as
> my own life ... May Heaven bless you
> prays your
> Nelson and Bronte

"Bronte" was the title of the dukedom Nelson had been awarded by a grateful King Ferdinand for his recapture of Naples from the French in 1799. Bronte, in Sicily, was a large estate, which should have yielded Nelson a good income but was, in reality, something of a white elephant. No matter: Nelson adored titles and honours.

Nelson had more to write before the fighting began. He sent messages to Captain Thomas Hardy, his second-in-command on *Victory*, and to Captain Henry Blackwood, commanding the *HMS Euryalus*, asking them to come and confer with him. While he waited, he took a fresh sheet of paper and carefully set out a codicil to his existing will. Its key sentence read:

> I leave Emma Lady Hamilton... a Legacy
> to my King and Country, that they will
> give her an ample provision to maintain her
> rank in life.

He also asked that his nation should look after Horatia, his "adopted daughter" – a polite fiction that few believed, but many accepted. Blackwood and Hardy came in, and Nelson modestly asked them if they would be good enough to sign themselves witnesses to the document. They obliged.

It was now 7.00 AM. The two fleets were moving with painful slowness towards engagement. Below decks, the sailors prepared their guns and the surgeons readied themselves to treat the many wounded men they expected. One aspect of their preparation was at Nelson's direct orders: they warmed their knives and other instruments to body temperature. Nelson had discovered that the pain of amputation was worse when the metal was cold.

At 8.00 AM, Villeneuve finally overcame his typical indecision and signalled to his ships that they should give up their movement south, turn about, reverse the order of sail (so that the last ship was now the first and vice versa), and take a northerly course – towards the shelter of Cádiz. In short, he was ordering a retreat.

Nelson did not like this development – not because he thought that Villeneuve had any real chance to escape, but because the approaches to Cádiz, always difficult even in moderate weather, would be perilous in the extreme when the gathering storm hit them. Those who did not die in battle might drown in its wake.

Villeneuve's order dismayed his own side. Commodore Cosme Damián de Churruca y Elorza, in charge of the *San Juan Nepomuncio*, read the signal and turned to one of his officers: "The fleet is doomed. The French admiral does not know his business. He has compromised us all!" He lowered his telescope and walked across the quarterdeck, muttering: *"Perdidos, perdidos, perdidos"* – "We are lost."

He summoned his crew to prayers.

Nelson was also moved to compose a prayer. He went back down to his cabin, took out his private diary and wrote some of the most famous words of his life – which were also the last written words of his life.

Monday, Octr. 21ˢᵗ, 1805.

May the Great God whom I worship
Grant to my Country and for the benefit
of Europe in General a great and Glorious
Victory, and may no misconduct in anyone
tarnish it, and may humanity after Victory
be the predominant feature in the British
Fleet. For myself individually I commit
my life to Him Who made me, and may
His blessing light upon my endeavours for
serving my Country faithfully. To Him I
resign myself and the just cause which is
entrusted to me to Defend. Amen, Amen,
Amen.

To twenty-first century readers, Nelson might seem to be displaying a hypocritical degree of piety here, yet it was undoubtedly sincere. However unconventional he was in the sphere of naval combat, he was profoundly traditional in most respects. His was the untroubled faith of his fathers and forefathers. One reason why he so hated the French is that he considered them faithless regicides who had murdered their Heavenly King as well as their National King.

Nelson rose, put on his best uniform and decorations, locked away his favourite portrait of Emma so that it should not be damaged, and went up to the poop deck. (An odd detail: in almost every other major engagement of his life, he wore his sword, but on this morning, he forgot it.) Out of his uniform, Nelson was not a particularly impressive sight: apart from his missing arm (lost at the Battle of Santa Cruz de Tenerife, 1797) and useless eye (wounded during action in Corsica, 1793), he was thin, gaunt and obviously damaged by years of illness and hardship. But in full dress, in his blue jacket, many bright decorations that dazzled in direct sunlight, and other colourful trappings, he was nonetheless magnificent – and also a glaringly visible target for enemy snipers. Afterwards, it was rumoured that his men would have preferred him to be less conspicuous – but no one had the moral fibre to suggest it. This was Nelson's way.

By about 10.00 AM, Villeneuve's fleet was stretched out in an approximate crescent formation, with some ships grouped closely together, some overlapping, and some far apart. Every gap in the line was a vulnerable point.

At 11.15, Villeneuve gave the signal: "Open fire as soon as the enemy is within range." Perhaps to his surprise, the Spanish and particularly the French roared with enthusiasm – the French cheering for their Emperor, the Spanish for their King. They were ready to fight.

When the opposing fleets were just half a mile away, Nelson turned to his signal officer, Lieutenant John Pasco. Pasco recorded the exchange:

> His Lordship ... said. "Mr. Pasco, I wish to say to the fleet, ENGLAND CONFIDES THAT EVERY MAN WILL DO HIS DUTY", and he added, "You must be quick, for I have one more to make which is for close action." I

replied, "If your Lordship will permit me to substitute the *confides* for *expects*, the signal will soon be completed, because the word *expects* is in the [signals] vocabulary, and *confides* must be spelt." His Lordship replied, in haste, and with seeming satisfaction, "That will do, Pasco, make it directly."

The now-famous order was not, on the whole, well received. Vice Admiral Cuthbert Collingwood, aboard the *HMS Royal Sovereign* was impatient: "What is Nelson signalling about? We all know what we have to do ...."

The sentiment was much the same between decks. One Lieutenant Ellis, a Marine Officer aboard the *HMS Ajax*, recalled:

Jack [i.e. the British Sailor, commonly known as "Jack Tar"] ... did not appreciate it, for there were murmurs from some, whilst others in an audible whisper said, "Do your duty! Of course we'll do our duty. I've always done mine, haven't you?"

But, the lieutenant went on:

"Still they cheered, more, I believe, from love and admiration for their admiral than from an appreciation of this well-known signal."

If the sailors did not admire the wording, Napoleon did. Some weeks later, having heard of the signal being flown in battle, he ordered that the ships of his own navy should all carry the inscription: *"La France Compte que chacun fera son Devoir."*

At 11.55 am, the British saw an explosion from the black hole of the *Fougueux*: the enemy had opened fire.

The Battle of Trafalgar had begun.

Chapter One

Youth (1758-77)

B ritain's hero was born on 29 September 1758 in Burnham Thorpe, a modest, remote village near the north
coast of Norfolk. His father, Rev. Edmund Nelson, was the
rector of Burnham Thorpe, and the Nelson family lived in
the parsonage. Horatio was a frail infant, so delicate that his
parents feared he might not survive, and hurried to have him
christened ten days after birth. He was the sixth child and
fifth son; the first, second and tenth of the Nelson offspring
all died in infancy. But Horatio proved more robust than he
looked, and though he remained small and slight all his life
and suffered from many illnesses, he had an iron will and
shrugged off all afflictions, rarely complaining.

Though respectable, the Nelson family was, at the best
of times, only modestly well-off, and, as clergymen were
not well paid, they often felt the financial pinch. Horatio's mother, Catherine Nelson, was from a grander family
than her husband. She was the daughter of Dr Maurice
Suckling, Prebendary of Westminster, who was himself

descended from the sister of Sir Robert Walpole, First Minister to the early Georges. The second Lord Walpole, Horace, was Horatio's godfather, and it was from him that "Horatio" was derived; in his early years, the boy preferred to be known by the less affected "Horace", and most members of his family called him by the English version.

Various branches of the Suckling family were substantial landowners throughout East Anglia, and it was Horatio's wealthy uncle Captain Maurice Suckling who sponsored the lad's bid to join the Royal Navy.

Horatio's mother died when he was just nine, during the bitterly cold Christmas of 1767. Some boys can take such early bereavement in their stride; others can be wounded for life. At first glance, Nelson seems to have survived the emotional wound unscathed. As an adult, he was decisive, self-confident to the point of recklessness and remarkably independent, almost entirely lacking in the conventional neuroses. But there were two great weaknesses in his character, which were to pain his friends and give glee to his enemies.

First, he was vain to the point of folly, with an unappeasable appetite for flattery and formal honours. Part of his intense ambition was a craving for medals, titles and all the standard paraphernalia of formal acclaim; wealth, which could come in abundance to successful captains in the form of generous prizes for the taking of enemy ships, held its obvious appeal to him, but recognition and praise were the rewards for which he truly hungered.

Second, in later life, was his grand passion for Emma Hamilton, which, touchy though he was, left him quite blind to the fact that many thought he was making himself utterly ridiculous. Whatever the basis of this *amour fou* – and part of it must have been the revelation of, at last, being loved by a beautiful and highly sexed woman – it is clear that Emma finally satisfied a chronic hunger in him that had never before been met – certainly not by his wife, Fanny. (Fanny also failed to praise him in the way he needed to be praised, while Emma's flatteries bordered on idolatry.) Early deprivation of maternal love is certainly not the full explanation for these related passions, but it can hardly be ignored.

After their mother's premature death, it became imperative that the children should be sent off to fend for themselves as soon as possible. Horatio, the only one of them eventually to earn fame and riches, decided to join the Navy, and asked his father to seek the sponsorship of his Uncle Maurice. Captain Suckling responded in a darkly joshing manner: "What had poor Horatio done, who is so weak, that he, above all the rest, should be sent to rough it out at sea?" But, he continued, "… let him come, and the first time we go into action, a cannon ball may knock off his head, and provide for him at once."

And so, on the first day of 1771, he joined his first ship at Chatham, the *Raisonnable*, of which Uncle Maurice was the captain. His uncle was away on business, and Horatio's first days on board were lonely and miserable. He was only twelve – not exceptionally young for the time, though there are signs that the adult Nelson came to think that it was: once, when he heard a midshipman at his table say that he had first seen active service in the Mediterranean at the age of eleven, Nelson murmured, "Too young …"

After about a year of service on the *Raisonnable*, Captain Suckling decided that the lad might benefit from a spell aboard a commercial West India ship. Horatio was seconded to the merchant shipping firm of Hibbert, Purrier and Horton, and despatched to Trinidad and Tobago on a ship captained by John Rathbone, who had served under Suckling on the *HMS Dreadnought*. It was a positive experience, on the whole, and confirmed the boy in his belief that he was suited for a life at sea. It also gave him an understanding of the feelings of the merchant marines, which made him far more sympathetic to their cause than was common among officers who had only known military seamanship.

One of these feelings was a suspicion of the naval mentality:

> If I did not improve my education, I
> returned a practical seaman, with a horror
> of the Royal Navy, and with a saying
> then constant with the seamen, "Aft the
> most honour, forward the better man." It
> was many weeks before I got in the least
> reconciled to a Man-of-War, so deep was
> the prejudice rooted; and what pains were
> taken to instil this erroneous principle in a
> young mind!

He rejoined the Navy, first as captain's servant and then as a midshipman with the *HMS Triumph*. In 1773, he heard that two Navy ships, the *Racehorse* and the *Carcass*, were being fitted out to make scientific observations in the Arctic Circle. When he first volunteered to join the expedition, he was refused; boys were deemed of no use, and were not to be employed. Horatio begged the captain of the *Carcass*, Skeffington Lutwidge, to let him join the crew doing a man's job: that of cockswain. So persistent were his pleas that Lutwidge eventually caved in; he did not regret his decision, and the two became close friends.

Carcass was thwarted on its journey north by the density of the pack ice it met, and was judged a scientific failure; but it offered Horatio ample scope to show his pluck. Early in July, the crew spotted curious lights in the sky – reflections from the ice floes ahead – and then the floes themselves. In the distance, they could see weird creatures, some kind of Northern 'monsters'. The crew set out to investigate in a pair of small boats, and when they soon encountered the walruses they had spotted, they opened fire with muskets. Two of the enraged creatures slithered off the ice to attack. They crashed into both sides of the boat with such immense force that they almost stove them in. But a second boat drew up, commanded by Midshipman Nelson, who gallantly drove the beasts away with oars.

Not long after this first encounter with Arctic wildlife, Nelson took himself off on another hazardous exploit. In later years, Captain Lutwidge enjoyed telling the story of how, one night, Nelson and one of his shipmates got it into their heads to sneak off the ship and hunt for a polar bear. Nelson led the way, musket in hand, fearlessly jumping over chasms in the ice. A fog began to descend, and the two lads were discovered missing. Lutwidge sent the signal for the truants to return, but Nelson ignored it. He was aiming his musket at a large bear separated from him only by a gap in the ice. Then he fired, but the musket failed. "No matter," exclaimed Nelson, "do but let me get a blow at the devil with the butt end of my musket, and we shall have him!"

Lutwidge ordered a blank charge to be fired. The bear loped away, and Nelson came back to the ship. There he was roundly told off for his truancy, and asked why on Earth he had been on a bear hunt. "Sir, I wished to kill the bear, that I might carry its skin to my father," he replied. Lutwidge decided not to punish such a spirited adventurer.

Soon the short Arctic summer came to an end, and they sailed back to England. Nelson later heard of a squadron that was being fitted out for a journey to the East, and felt strongly that

> ... nothing less than such a distant voyage
> could in the least satisfy my desire of
> maritime knowledge; and I was placed
> in the *Seahorse* of 20 guns, with Captain
> Farmer, and watched in the foretop:
> from whence in time I was placed on the
> quarter-deck, having, in the time I was
> in this ship, visited almost every part of
> the East Indies, from Bengal to Bussorah
> [Basra].

It was on this mission that he had his first taste of naval combat – a minor skirmish off the Malabar coast.

In Bombay, during the last weeks of 1775, Nelson contracted a severe fever. He came so close to death that the surgeon of the *Salisbury* pronounced that his only hope of survival was to be sent home to England. He was transferred to the *Dolphin*, which, on 23 March 1776, began the slow journey home – more than six months. Nelson suffered badly on the way, not only from his illness but from savage bouts of depression. This affliction came back to plague him several times in his career, and gave him as much distress as any wound or fever.

Then came something that Nelson believed, for the rest of his life, was a miracle. He had a "vision" of a glowing orb floating in the air in front of him. He regarded it as a message from God, and it sustained him throughout the darkest passages of his perilous career.

He recovered so well for the rest of the journey that by the time the *Dolphin* docked at Woolwich on 24 September 1776, he was almost immediately given a new assignment – as lieutenant of the *Worcester,* a ship of the line armed with sixty-four guns. His first mission was escort duty for ships sailing to Gibraltar.

On 9 April 1777, Nelson took his captain's examination. His uncle, Maurice Suckling, was on the board, but kept his family connection to the young man secret until the other officers showed that they had been suitably impressed by the candidate: "I did not wish the younker to be favoured. I felt convinced that he would pass a good examination; and you see, gentlemen, that I have not been disappointed."

It seems likely that this was little more than a favourite family yarn. At any rate, it was quite unlikely that the panel would not have been well aware of the family connection. Still, young Horatio had done well. The possibility of a distinguished naval career, and all the riches it might bring, was now open to him.

Chapter Two

Early Navy Years (1778-86)

Nelson's first posting, to the frigate *Lowestofte*, was both happy and life-changing. The ship's captain was William Locker, who became something of an affectionate mentor to the youth, and then a friend. The two remained on excellent terms until Locker's death twenty-three years later. It was Locker who urged Nelson, in the spell of shore leave he was allowed before the *Lowestofte* set sail for Jamaica, to attend the London studio of the artist John Francis Rigaud and have his first portrait done. Rigaud duly set to work, but put the canvas aside for about four years until Nelson came back and could sit again. Nelson was just eighteen when Rigaud began, and the completed portrait, which became well-known, is by far the best likeness of him we have in the years before his appearance was made harsher by wounds and anxiety.

When they set sail, Locker put Nelson in charge of the "Little Lucy" – the tender boat for the *Lowestofte*. Nelson reflected with due pride that "[i]n this vessel, I made myself a complete pilot for all the passages through the Islands situated on the north side of Hispaniola" – that is, modern-day Haiti and the Dominican Republic. Hispaniola was at this time a French possession, and France's ships were now beginning to patrol both American waters as well as West Indian waters in growing numbers.

On the same day, 8 December, a Northumbrian called Cuthbert Collingwood was made second lieutenant of the *Lowestofte*. Though the temperaments of these two young officers could hardly have been more opposed, they, too, were soon to become good friends, and they remained so until the Battle of Trafalgar, in which Collingwood commanded the *Royal Sovereign*.

It became increasingly clear on both sides of the Atlantic that war was coming. It finally did come on 6 February 1778, when the British government declared war on France. The aspect of this action that mattered most to Nelson was the possibility of an imminent French attack on Jamaica – the richest of Britain's colonies in the West Indies. Jamaica was put on alert, and, in the summer of 1778, Sir Peter Parker arrived there to become Commander-in-Chief. As many older men had done, Parker took a shine to young Nelson and arranged for his rapid promotion. On 8 December of that year, he was made commander and appointed to the *Badger*, which was "sent to protect the Mosquito shore, and the bay of Honduras, from the depredations of the American [and other] privateers". To use their modern names, Nelson's range of patrol was from southern Mexico, Guatemala, Honduras, Nicaragua, and Costa Rica.

On 11 June 1779, Nelson was promoted post-captain (that is, Captain in all but official title) and appointed to the frigate *Hinchingbrooke*, a thirty-two-gun ship whose previous captain had been killed by a random shot. This was a crucial moment in Nelson's early career. If he managed to avoid being killed, he was now virtually guaranteed to be made a full Captain.

Just a few days later, on 16 June, Spain declared war on Britain; there were now three enemy nations to confront. In September, the Spanish opened hostilities by raiding a British settlement on the coast of Honduras. The British retaliated with a highly profitable raid on a Spanish settlement, Omoa, where they took possession of a fortune in Guatamalan gold. This triumph made the British mood bullish: they began to lay plans for further raids, and for large-scale land grabs of extensive and weakly defended territories. It now seemed possible that "New Spain" might be sliced in two, with British troops stationed between Mexico and Peru. Major-General John Dalling, in charge of the British forces, proposed that this process should begin with an invasion of Nicaragua, and the British government approved this bold scheme.

The invasion was mainly a land operation, but the Navy would need to be involved, too – troop ships would have to be escorted to the mouth of the San Juan, up which they would proceed to Lake Nicaragua. Dalling knew just the man for the job: the reliable Horatio Nelson. Few could have foreseen that this appointment would very nearly be the death of the Captain.

The invasion formally began in February 1780, when the armed fleet sailed from Kingston; it anchored of the mouth of the San Juan River. Strictly speaking, this completed Nelson's part in the operation; his orders were to remain there until relieved. The British fleet established a camp on shore, and prepared their canoes for the river journey. The larger ones were of two types: the *panga*, about forty feet long, which could carry sixteen tons of cargo, and the *pipante,* about half the size. Each carried smaller boats.

All seemed well in principle, but when the men tried to row their boats from the sea into the river, the result was chaos. Strong currents tossed the boats violently about. One capsized, and then another, and within minutes there was little to be seen but upturned and split boats, sinking cargo and men thrashing about for their lives in wild waters. Nelson saw at once that what they needed was a sailor richly experienced in river navigation – that is, himself. Much to the relief and gratitude of his superiors, he volunteered to take over command.

With the flotilla now stripped down to basics, the invasion began again. Under Nelson's command, the small ships now made better progress, though not without struggle. Many of the crafts ran into sand and other obstructions, and even when the whole flotilla was finally in the river, the troubles did not cease. The faster ships were soon far ahead of the slower ones. For the next few days, they progressed by little more than a couple of miles each day, suffering from intense heat by day and unexpected cold at nights.

When they had finally covered about six miles, their Indian scouts reported back that there was a Spanish battery not far ahead. A body of troops was sent ashore, and soon the men discovered quite how hostile the territory was. Their clothes were torn and stripped from them by branches and roots; black leeches fastened to their bodies and grew plump with blood. One soldier was bitten in the eye by a snake, and let out a dreadful scream. He died almost at once, and within a couple of hours his corpse was already putrefying.

Despite these horrors, Nelson launched an attack on the Spanish battery and, stumbling through thick mud while brandishing his sword as the musket-balls whizzed past him, soon forced the enemy to surrender. From their captives, they learned that their prime objective, the Castle of San Juan, was only five miles upstream. Nelson was all for making an immediate and decisive attack, but his immediate superior, Captain John Polson, had learned that reinforcements were now on their way up the river. Better, Polson thought, to wait for them and then begin a siege.

The attack was finally launched on 11 April. The commander of the Spanish fortress, Don Juan d'Ayssa, saw the British boats round the river, and gave the order to his men to lock down for a siege. When the firing began, Nelson operated his own cannon and proved an excellent artilleryman: his very first shot brought down the Spanish flag. But the advantage could not be pushed home; first, because so much ammunition had been lost in accidents on the way upriver, but mainly because the seasonal rains had begun. The power of the torrent was staggering: tents and huts were beaten down and smashed, and visibility was reduced to virtually nil.

The reinforcements arrived in the middle of the deluge. Its commander was all for Nelson's idea of a direct frontal assault, and the cautious Polson finally gave in. By the 28th, all the materials for an attack were in place, and Polson made the Spanish an offer: surrender or we attack. But then new despatches arrived: 500 more troops had been despatched from Jamaica, and were already beginning their trip upriver. A private despatch for Nelson informed him that he had been appointed captain of the frigate *Janus* and was to pass command of the *Hinchinbroke* over to Collingwood.

There was one practical difficulty. Like so many of the British force, Nelson had been stricken by both dysentery and malaria, and was stretched out in his tent, gravely ill. It was by no means sure that he could survive the efforts of a journey back downriver. Nevertheless, he was dragged onto a canoe and pushed off in the direction of the coast.

He somehow survived this latest trial, and on 1 May his canoe reached the British anchorage. It should have been a heartening sight, but it was not: at least half the crew on board Nelson's frigate were dangerously ill with fever, and the other ships were also gravely depleted. Collingwood was shocked at Nelson's hollow, yellow features, and dismayed to hear that the castle of San Juan had still not been taken – it had been widely assumed that the British had enjoyed an easy victory. Command of the ship was duly transferred, and Nelson was taken back to Jamaica. His condition was judged so severe that Admiral William Cornwallis insisted that he avoid hospital and be cared for by his former slave and presumed lover, an experienced and well-respected traditional healer tactfully known as Cubah Cornwallis (as if the couple were legally married). Cubah's remedies and her affectionate, optimistic coddling of Nelson saw him through the worst of his illness. Without her, he probably would have died.

On 2 June, word came that the British had finally taken San Juan. It was widely held among the officer classes in Jamaica that a great deal of death and suffering might have been spared if Polson had only been brave or even sensible and followed Nelson's original advice. Nelson himself was careful to praise Polson's conduct.

Nelson spent weeks in recuperation. His recovery was slow, and he still struck visitors as gravely ill. His favourite clinician, the erudite and somewhat eccentric Dr Mosely, doubted that he was well enough to take command of the *Janus,* and recommended that he should do nothing more than convalesce. But Nelson still dreamed of being a part in the great conflict on the Spanish Main, and of achieving a triumph that would make him part of history.

Then came dreadful news. An English colonel at the head of further reinforcements had visited Polson's troops and was horrified by what he found. Almost all of them were sick with dysentery, malaria, or both, and many had died. Worse, his own reinforcements almost immediately came down with the same illnesses, and, struggle as the doctors might, were also dying on all sides. A final estimate of the catastrophe held that of the 2,000 or so men sent upriver between February and November, barely 100 survived. In addition, more than 1,000 of the sailors anchored near the river had died. On Collingwood's new command, the *Hinchinbroke,* only ten out of 200 had survived.

By this time, Nelson was on a ship back to England. Still weak and at times in extreme pain, he arrived back in England in the autumn of 1780. After a brief spell meeting friends in and around London, he went to Bath for the winter, partly because it was warmer than the capital (Bath, he wrote to Locker, "is like Jamaica to any other part of England"), and partly to recover from his various complaints. The treatments were of some help, but he was worried about an intermittent paralysis that struck his left arm and leg. The Admiralty assured him that in due course he would be offered another ship; but for the time being, he was to continue to convalesce as patiently as he could manage.

In the summer of 1781, Nelson paid a visit to his family in Burnham Thorpe. He was somewhat alarmed when his brother William, now a curate and obviously more than a little jealous of Horatio's adventurous career, spoke about going to sea himself as a naval chaplain. Horatio tried to discourage him, but to little effect.

By 23 August, Nelson was judged well enough to take over his next command, the *Albemarle*, of twenty-eight guns. As the war to preserve the American colonies had required many Navy ships to protect Atlantic convoys, there was a serious shortage of vessels and even more of men to look after British interests in the English Channel and the Baltic Sea. This was to be Nelson's new responsibility, and to carry it out he would be obliged to press men from the merchant marine. He did so with complete ruthlessness, and opened fire on some East Indiamen near the Thames estuary.

The next call was Denmark, where the *Albemarle* was treated with some coolness until Nelson asserted his – and Britain's – right to a ceremonial welcome. Then, in January 1782, an East Indiaman accidentally crashed into his vessel, damaging her so badly that she had to sail to Portsmouth for major repairs. She was out of action until the start of April, when Nelson was ordered back across the Atlantic. There, in the revolutionary United States of America, the British were on the brink of defeat. Nelson's orders were to escort a convoy from Cork to the mouth of the St Lawrence River in Canada, and then to patrol the coast between Cape Cod and Boston in search of French or American fighting ships.

The most memorable event of his first weeks off the American coast came when he took a schooner, the *Harmony*, whose American captain Nathaniel Carver held firmly pro-British views. Nelson was impressed by the man's seamanship, and recruited him as a pilot for these difficult waters. Carver's knowledge and skills proved invaluable when they were attacked by French ships. After nine hours of ingenious manoeuvring, the French gave up the pursuit. Nelson was delighted, and told Carver:

> You have rendered us, Sir, a very useful
> service, and it is not the custom of English
> seamen to be ungrateful. In the name,
> therefore, and with the approbation of
> the Officers of this Ship, I return your
> Schooner, and with it this certificate of
> your good conduct. Farewell! and may God
> bless you.

Carver in his turn admired Nelson, and shortly after his release sailed back to the ship with sacks of vegetables, poultry and four sheep for the benefit of the sailors, who had begun to suffer from scurvy.

Nelson's next order was to Quebec, where all the men suffering from scurvy were sent to hospital, and the rest immediately given fresh food and drink. Nelson found that the climate was well suited to him, and restored him to the health he had enjoyed before the Nicaraguan campaign. He wrote to his father:

> Health, that greatest of blessings, is
> what I never truly enjoyed till I saw fair
> Canada. The change it has wrought, I am
> convinced, is truly wonderful.

From this point until his marriage a few years later, the previously unromantic Horatio began a series of flirtations and dalliances; he reports having fallen in love with an almost comic frequency. It seems probable that his new role as swain was inspired by more than simple amorousness: an ambitious young post-captain was in need of a suitable wife. The first target of his affections was one Mary Simpson, the handsome sixteen-year old daughter of the Provost-Marshal of the Quebec garrison. But Nelson's new friend, a rich merchant and councillor by the name of Alexander Davison, at first discouraged and then forbade him from proposing marriage.

The *Albemarle's* next destination was New York. There Nelson met a young midshipman, Prince William Henry, later to be King William IV. The two men made a favourable impression on each other; the prince thought Nelson "no common being". Nelson's orders took him back to the waters near Jamaica, where he captured a French merchantman (but had to share the £20,000 prize with the rest of the fleet under Rear-Admiral [later Lord] Samuel Hood, as the fleet had been in view); then, in March, he badly mismanaged an assault on a French base in the Bahamas. He might have faced a court-martial had it not been for the news that a ceasefire had been declared, so that peace negotiations could take place. Instead of being tried, he was sent back to England, and no more was said.

On 11 July, Hood took Nelson to a levee at St James, where he was warmly received by George III. On the whole, Nelson was content with the outcome of his recent trials: "I have closed the war without a fortune, but I trust, and ... believe that there is not a speck on my character."

There was now an interval of peace between England and France. In October 1783, Nelson did a surprising thing. This lifelong foe of France set off across the Channel for a pleasure trip. At first, his distaste for the French as an inferior people was confirmed. He found most of the country ugly and its inns squalid beyond anything he had experienced, but when he finally reached the town of Saint-Omer, he was pleasantly taken by its cleanliness and order. Here, he flirted inexpertly with French girls – he never learned to speak their language – and then, predictably, fell in love with an English girl, Miss Andrews. He thought seriously of marrying her, and described her in a letter home as

> [a]n English young lady, the daughter of a
> clergyman ... She has such accomplishments
> that, had I a million of money, I am sure
> I should make her an offer of them; my
> income at present is by far too small to
> think of marriage, and she has no fortune.

And so he wrote to his uncle, William Suckling, asking for financial support in his effort to become a married gentleman. William agreed, but by this time Horatio had learned that Miss Andrews had no immediate intentions to marry any man, let alone an impecunious sailor.

Holidays over, Horatio returned to London to find the capital in a state of high political excitement in the aftermath of Britain losing her American colonies. Nelson's political allegiances at this time were somewhat divided between the traditional Tory loyalties of his father's family and the Whig values of his prosperous relatives on his mother's side. He was to grow more Conservative with the years, and was a great admirer of the youthful new prime minister, William Pitt the Younger, who was only twenty-five. For a few weeks he even dabbled with the idea of standing for Parliament himself; but before he could make much of an effort in this direction, the Admiralty summoned him back to duty.

On 18 March 1784, Lord Howe, one of the great figures of the Navy, appointed Nelson to a frigate of twenty-eight guns, the *Boreas*, named after the Classical term for the North Wind. His first mission was to the Leeward Islands Station, where his most important passenger, Sir Richard Hughes, was to take up the post of Commander-in-Chief. Sir Richard was accompanied by his wife and a daughter. Nelson was not pleased with their company; he thought Lady Hughes a tiresome chatterbox – an "eternal clack" – and her daughter, plain and dull. Nor did he much care for Sir Richard, whom he thought sycophantic – "he bows and scrapes too much" – and faintly ridiculous. Sir Richard lacked one eye – not from a wound incurred in action, but from the ludicrous accident of having somehow stabbed himself with a fork while chasing a cockroach.

Another passenger was Horatio's brother William, who still had his heart set on a career as a naval chaplain, despite a conspicuous lack of piety and theological learning. He had managed to wear down Horatio's valiant attempts to deter him from a life at sea.

The voyage looked likely to end almost as soon as it had begun, as the pilot from Chatham managed to run *Boreas* aground. Still, as annoying as Lady Hughes was to Nelson, she did keep a lively record of the journey. She noted, in particular, Nelson's thoughtful and encouraging care of his midshipmen, whom he called his "children". There were about thirty lads, and, as Lady Hughes recalled:

> Among the number it may reasonably be
> supposed that there must be timid as well
> as bold: the timid he never rebuked, but
> always wished to show them he desired
> nothing of them that he would not instantly

do himself: and I have known him to say –
"Well, Sir, I am going a race to the mast-
head, and beg I may meet you there!"

No denial could be given to such a wish,
and the poor fellow instantly began his
march. His Lordship never took the least
notice with what alacrity it was done, but
when he met at the top, began instantly
speaking in the most cheerful manner, and
saying how much a person was to be pitied
who could fancy there was any danger, or
even anything disagreeable, in the attempt.
After this excellent example, I have seen
the timid youth lead another, and rehearse
his Captain's words. How wise and kind
was such a proceeding! ...

By June they had reached Madeira, and by the end of
September they were harboured at Antigua. Nelson
considered the island's shipyard, long neglected and in
disrepair, an "infernal hole". He was in a bad temper and
starved of intelligent, congenial company. His brother,
thinking the climate bad for his health, soon left. The
one social comfort for him, until his friend Collingwood
sailed into harbour in November, was a Mrs Moutray, wife
of the Commander of the Navy on the island, who struck
him as quite remarkable – so much so that he wrote to
his sister Kate that he hoped she and Mrs Moutray would
one day meet: "What an acquisition to any female to be
acquainted with; what an example to take pattern from."

But he found his superiors almost insufferable. "The
Admiral and all about him are great ninnies," he said, and

Hughes had already struck him as a toady. It was in this sour frame of mind that Nelson began a course of action that earned him many enemies. Simply put, he decided that he would enforce to the full the terms of the Navigation Act, which aimed to control trade in the area: goods being taken either to or from Colonial territories must be carried either in the ships of those colonies or British ones. The success of the American War of Independence meant that men and women who had formerly been British subjects were now aliens, with no British rights. But, as Nelson put it, "… [t]he Americans, when colonists, possessed almost all the trade from America to our West India Islands; and on the return of Peace, they forgot … they had become foreigners, and of course had no right to trade in the British colonies".

In reality, it suited the local governors and custom house officers to turn a blind eye and allow trade to continue as it had. Having announced his intention to crack down, Nelson set about seizing the offending vessels. This outraged everyone who was profiting, and rage against Nelson was so intense that he did not dare put into harbour anywhere for fear of being mobbed. But he was stubborn: he feared that if the illegal trade were permitted to thrive, it would lead to further defections from Britain:

> I, for one, am determined not to suffer the Yankees to come where my Ship is; for I am sure, if once the Americans are admitted to any kind of intercourse with these Islands the views of the Loyalists [i.e., those loyal to Britain] are entirely done away. They will become first the Carriers, and next have possession of our Islands,

> are we ever again embroiled in a French
> war. The residents of these Islands are
> Americans by connexion and by interest,
> and are inimical to Great Britain. They are
> as great rebels as ever were in America,
> had they the power to show it.

This grim assessment was almost certainly right. In March, he had to refuse an invitation from the president of St Kitts, because the rebellious Irish had raised their colours all over the island to celebrate St Patrick's Day; and some months later, a French frigate taunted the *Boreas* by sailing closely by, to leeward. Nelson pursued them and boarded the ship to make his intentions plain, in pointedly civil but unambiguous words. He declared that it would be his honour to escort the French vessel around the Islands for as long as it remained. The French commander caught his drift, and the ship set off for Martinique, shadowed as far as Barbados by Nelson.

The French were not Nelson's only antagonists. General Shirley, Governor of the Leeward Islands, who was keen that the illegal trade should continue, tried to pull rank on Nelson, telling him that he was far too young and inexperienced to tell his betters what they should do. Nelson angrily pointed out that he was the same age as Prime Minister Pitt, and that he considered himself as capable of commanding one of His Majesty's ships as Mr Pitt was in commanding the ship of State. Nelson's former passenger, Sir Richard Hughes, was inclined to take Shirley's side, until he discovered that more and more officers were taking the view that Nelson was in the right.

The affair came to an unpleasant head when Nelson seized four American ships anchored off the coast of Nevis, a rich British possession with eighty sugar plantations. The island's merchant class was outraged, and wanted sue Nelson for damages, to the vast sum of £40,000. He was warned that if he dared to step ashore, he would be arrested and imprisoned.

But, to his relief, the local authorities backed him. The judge at the courthouse of Nevis's capital, Charlestown, ruled that Nelson was entirely within his rights to seize the offending ships, and President John Herbert of Nevis said that he would put up £10,000 in bail for Nelson should any arrest be attempted. Nelson and Herbert soon became close friends, and Nelson was invited to stay in Herbert's large, handsome house, Montpelier.

How did Nelson appear to the local, wealthy civilians at this time? A letter from a young woman who had been seated next to him at a formal dinner suggests that he struck them as grim and aloof:

> We have at last seen the Captain of the *Boreas*, of whom so much has been said. He came up just before dinner, much heated, and was very silent; yet seemed, according to the old adage, to think the more. He declined drinking any wine; but after dinner, when the President, as usual, gave the following toasts, "the King", "the Queen and Royal Family", and "Lord Hood", this strange man regularly filled his glass, and observed, that those were always bumper toasts with him; which having drank, he uniformly passed the bottle, and relapsed into his former taciturnity. It was impossible, during this visit, for any of us to

make out his real character; there was such
a reserve and sternness in his behaviour,
with occasional sallies, though very transient,
of a superior mind. Being placed by him,
I endeavoured to rouse his attention by
showing him all the civilities in my power;
but I drew out little more than "Yes"
or "No". If you, Fanny, had been there,
we think you would have made something
of him; for you have been in the habit of
attending to these odd sort of people.

The "Fanny" addressed here was Frances Herbert Nisbet, who was the niece of Mr Herbert and the daughter of William Woodford, Senior Judge of Nevis. Her late husband Josiah had been a doctor, and she had borne him a son, who was also named Josiah; but Dr Nevis, long an invalid, had died just eighteen months after the birth. Fanny had by then been a widow for four years. In fact, it was the five-year-old Josiah who first met Nelson; the fierce commander of whom so many were afraid adored children, and had joined the lad in spirited play under the dining-room table.

Fanny was a woman of parts: slender, with delicate features that, some thought, bore witness to her sorrows. She possessed all the accomplishments required of young ladies: she dressed and comported herself elegantly, could speak French (again, a language Nelson would never master) and ply a useful needle. They entered into a court-ship, taking long, sedate walks around Montpelier's agree-able gardens and grounds. The records suggest that their mating dance was more elegant than passionate, and it may have been that Nelson was so keen to find a wife that any other young lady on the island might have been just as attractive to him as Fanny. But he clearly thought she was intelligent as well as charming, and wrote that "her mental accomplishments are superior to most peoples of either sex".

Not everyone agreed with this. Years later, one of Nelson's midshipmen who had known her at the time recalled that

> ... she had at that time some beauty, and a
> freshness of complexion not common in that
> climate, but there was so remarkable an
> absence of intellectual endowment as to make
> it evident that Nelson's sagacious eye was
> content to dwell upon the blooming cheeks,
> without going in search of better graces
> which give permanence to conjugal felicity.

Whether or not this scathing judgement was just, there is no doubt that Nelson was determined on marriage. On 28 June 1785, he wrote to his brother from St Kitts: "*Entre Nous*, do not be surprised to hear that I am a Benedict, for if at all, it will be before a month. Do not tell."

By "Benedict" – an allusion to the hero of Shakespeare's *Much Ado About Nothing* – he meant that he intended, if possible, soon to be married. On 11 September, he wrote to Fanny:

> My greatest wish is to be united to
> you; and the foundation of all conjugal
> happiness, real love and esteem is, I trust,
> what you believe I possess in the strongest
> degree towards you.

She accepted his proposal of marriage, but he was back at sea again before Mr Herbert could give the union his formal approval. For the second time, Nelson wrote a begging letter to William Suckling, asking him for enough money to enable him to support Fanny in the comfortable manner to which she had grown accustomed in Nevis.

Nelson also wrote to Fanny several times in the months before their marriage. One of the letters was surprisingly playful and flirtatious for such a reserved man:

> Have you not often heard that salt water
> and absence always wash away love? Now,
> I am such a heretic as not to believe that
> faith; for, behold, every morning I have
> had six pails of salt water poured upon my
> head, and instead of finding what seamen
> say to be true, it goes on so contrary to the
> prescription, that you must, perhaps see me
> before the fixed time ...

During this interval before the wedding, Admiral Hughes had sailed for England, leaving Nelson as the temporary senior officer of the Leeward Islands station. In this capacity, Nelson now had to play host to Prince William Henry, who had been promoted to Post-Captain and given command of the frigate *Pegasus*. It was a pleasant and at times exhausting chore for Nelson, who dearly loved a royal, and consisted largely of accompanying the prince in a seemingly endless round of receptions, dinner parties, cockfights and balls, where he paid his customary attentions to pretty young ladies.

The prince, in his turn, greatly enjoyed the company of his more sober companion, and began to twit Nelson about the undue length of his engagement to Fanny. Eventually, he insisted not only that Nelson should be married by the time his stay was over, but that it should be he who would give the bride away. The ceremony duly took place on 11 March 1787.

In a letter to Locker shortly after the ceremony, Nelson wrote about his hope of returning to England on the *Boreas*:

> Happy shall I be when that times arrives
> [*sic*]. No man has had more illness
> or trouble on a Station than I have
> experienced: but let me lay a balance
> on the other side – I am married to an
> amiable woman, that far makes amends
> for everything: indeed, till I married her I
> never knew happiness. And I am morally
> certain she will continue to make me a
> happy man for the rest of my days.

Poor Nelson; and poorer Fanny.

Chapter Three

England, Corsica, Cape St Vincent

England: Five Years of Rejection

Nelson was not well-off. The Admiralty put him on half-pay: £53 12s 6d paid once every six months. Suckling gave him £100 a year, and the president of Nevis gave Fanny the same sum. On these modest means they travelled around England for about a year, visiting family and friends in London, Exmoor, Bath and Plymouth before returning to Horatio's boyhood home in Norfolk. They set up house at Burnham Thorpe.

Fanny, who hated cold weather, was miserable there, and would take to her bed for days at a time during the winter. Nelson's father noted that "Mrs. N. Takes large doses of the bed, and finds herself only comfortable when enclosed in moreen ..." Even the stoical Horatio, accustomed to the bleak Norfolk winters from his childhood, found the weather dispiriting, and felt his first rheumatic aches. Like his wife, he stayed indoors for the most part; unlike her, he occupied himself with reading (especially travel books) and examining naval charts. But when spring came, he threw himself into all manner of hobbies and occupations – digging the gardens, hunting for birds' eggs, and coursing hares.

But, more and more, he longed for another command:

> I made use of every interest to get a Ship, even a boat, to serve my Country, but in vain; there was a prejudice at the Admiralty evidently against me, which I can neither guess at, or in the least account for.

He could see that his skills would soon be needed again by his nation. At the height of summer, on 14 July 1789, the Bastille was stormed by a revolutionary mob, and the following month the National Constituent Assembly adopted the Declaration of the Rights of Man and of the Citizen. The French Revolution was a *fait accompli*. But if Nelson could see the trouble ahead, the Admiralty, apparently, did not. For the next five years, every one of his pleas to be given a ship was spurned by the Lords. So he cultivated his garden and read the news from France with deepening worry.

He was yet more disturbed by the possibility that the French revolutionary virus had spread to Britain – a fear felt by the propertied classes across Europe: "… the times are turbulent, and the enthusiasm for liberty is raging even to madness. The success of the French people in establishing their republic has set the same principle, which lurked in every state in Europe, afloat."

The Return
Everything changed at the start of 1793, when it became

obvious to the Admiralty as well as almost everyone else in England that the French were about to declare war again. Louis XVI was executed, and France's National Convention declared that it would offer "assistance to all people who wish to recover their liberty": in other words, if the oppressed classes of England wished to rise up against their rulers, the French would aid them. This was a grave misreading of the popular mood.

On 6 January, Nelson was finally summoned to London, and was justifiably flustered by the warmth with which he was greeted. He wrote to Fanny:

> The Admiralty so smile upon me that
> really, I am as much surprised as when they
> frowned. Lord Chatham yesterday made
> many apologies for not having given me a
> ship before this time and said that, if I chose
> to take a sixty-four to begin with, I should
> be appointed to one as soon as she was
> ready; and, whenever it was in his power, I
> should be removed into a seventy-four.

The sixty-four in question was the *Agamemnon*, in dock at Chatham. On 1 February 1793, France declared war on Britain. A week later, Nelson joined the *Agamemnon* – still being hastily prepared by teams of carpenters and other craftsmen, while its hull was being loaded with water and salt meat. Every day, new drafts of seamen arrived and were kitted out. Though everyone worked furiously, Nelson was champing at the bit, and his impatience sometimes made him ill-tempered. His letters home to Fanny crackled with irritation.

Finally, by the middle of April, the *Agamemnon* was

ready for sea. When she finally set sail down the coast to Spithead, the crew was still 100 men short. Nevertheless, Nelson was cheered. She was fast – perhaps the fastest in the Navy – and she handled well. He had planned to head out to sea as soon as possible, but gales prevented them, and most of the younger crew members were seasick. Once free of the storms, she engaged with some French ships, but inconclusively.

Nelson's next orders were to join the fleet headed by Lord Hood, aboard the *Victory*, bound for the Mediterranean. *Agamemnon* joined Hood's fleet on 11 May, sailing for Cádiz and the Strait of Gibraltar. For a brief interval, Britain's traditional enemy, Spain, was now an ally. Hood's primary mission was to blockade the ports of Marseilles and Toulon. This they did, for over a month, until the men on the ships were as starved of fresh food as their enemies.

Then, quite unexpectedly, Toulon – whose inhabitants were largely loyal to their late king – surrendered to Hood. Marseilles also tried to surrender, but a Republican army stormed in and exacted terrible punishment. The British takeover of Toulon was peaceful, but Nelson played no part in it. He was despatched on a diplomatic mission, to strengthen the eastern flank of operations against France by recruiting the support of the Kingdom of Naples. The kingdom was ruled by the Spanish Bourbon dynasty in the persons of King Ferdinand IV (later Ferdinand I of the Kingdom of the Two Sicilies) and Queen Maria Carolina, daughter of Empress Maria Theresa of Austria and sister of Marie Antoinette (who, at this time, was imprisoned). This meeting was one of most fateful of Nelson's life; or, as his biographer Robert Southey put it: "Thus that acquaintance began which ended in the destruction of Nelson's domestic happiness." No one could have predicted it, but perhaps the gods knew: as Nelson's ship sailed into the Bay of Naples on 10 September, 1793, Vesuvius erupted in a most spectacular manner. Nelson thought the spectacle "splendid".

Nelson first met William and Emma at the grandly appointed British embassy. The three took to each other at once. Several days later he met King Ferdinand, and watched him drill some 4,000 soldiers who would be placed under Nelson's command. The act seemed vainglorious to Nelson, whose attitude to the king grew increasingly sceptical. On 5 October he was back in Toulon, where the fighting was fierce. The French forces, strengthened by regular arrivals of reinforcements, killed many of the British and their allies.

On 16 October, Marie Antoinette was beheaded. When the news reached the Mediterranean, there were scenes of fury: Maria Carolina was driven almost insane with rage, and swore an oath of undying vengeance against her sister's murderers. Nelson engaged inconclusively with some French vessels, and then received word from Lord Hood that he should sail for Corsica and take charge of the fleet there. Not long after they arrived, he heard the dreadful news that Toulon – almost inevitably – had fallen to the French. Hood had managed to rescue some 15,000 residents, but then the town's defences collapsed. The French slaughtered indiscriminately.

January – August 1794: The Corsican Campaign

Nelson's next major task was to secure, as a replacement base, Corsica – birthplace of Napoleon, soon to become England's greatest enemy. It had been a French possession, but France had sold the island to Italy. There were still French forces on Corsica, many of them based in two major forts, Bastia and Calvi, on the east and west coasts. Although they were strongly defended, Nelson was confident that both could be taken from the sea. He was delighted with the calibre of his crew: "My ship's company behave most exceedingly well. They begin to look on themselves as invincible, almost invulnerable. They really mind shot no more than peas."

The campaign began with an attempt on Bastia – a difficult target, built with high walls and a strong citadel; to the south were swamps. Nelson landed 2,000 men at a beach some three miles north of the town. The preparations involved a heroic feat of engineering: the sailors hacked down trees, cleared rocks and built sledges on which heavy guns could be dragged into position. When all was ready, Hood came ashore and demanded surrender. The enemy commander, Jean-Pierre Lacombe St-Michel, defied him. Hood raised the red flag, and the artillery bombardments began.

Bastia took the worst of the pounding, and soon its defenders were also feeling the pangs of hunger. By 19 May, Bastia was ready to surrender. The British marched in to the sound of their bands playing patriotic airs, and the British colours were raised above the fortress. Nelson was exultant:

> At daylight this morning, the most glorious
> sight which an Englishman, and I believe
> none but an Englishman, could experience,
> was to be seen: 4,500 men laying down
> their arms to less than 1,000 English soldiers.

Next target: Calvi. This town was even more heavily fortified than Bastia, with vast granite walls that rose up directly from the rocks on the shore, while the coasts were so rocky that it was hard for ships to anchor. On 17 June the *Agamemnon* was anchored near Calvi, and Nelson made an assessment of the ground on which they would be fighting. It did not look promising, but he sent guns and troops ashore anyway. This arduous task was made all but impossible when a storm hit, sending the British ships out to sea and pinning down the shore force. When it lifted, the ground troops began a fortnight of dragging guns up to the place from which they would be fired, and building batteries. It was backbreaking, exhausting work.

Then, on 4 July, the firing began. It was dangerous work, and Nelson marvelled that the death toll among his men was as low as a handful every day. On 12 June, he became one of the casualties himself. While observing the fire, he was struck by fragments of a shell that burst nearby. His face was covered with cuts, but he made light of them. He told Hood: "I got a little hurt this morning, not much ..." But four days later he had to admit that his right eye had been seriously damaged. He could only make out patches of darkness and light, no shapes; three weeks later, he was forced to acknowledge that the use of his eye had gone forever.

This was not the only bad news. The men, exhausted from the hauling, fell sick from typhoid and dysentery as the summer heat grew intense. Soon, more than 1,000 men – half the force – were incapacitated, and the rest "not much better than phantoms". By the end of July, illness had all but defeated them, and Nelson could not determine how much longer they could maintain a siege. At this point, the French commander made an offer to surrender, after another twenty-five days, under certain conditions. It was clear that the British could not endure that long. Hood had two options: give up the siege, or make a full-on assault. When the British saw that some French relief ships had slipped through the blockade, they thought that Calvi could fight on for longer – though in fact the ships had brought food, not ammunition.

Ammunition was what the French desperately lacked. On 1 August, they therefore agreed to negotiate a surrender within ten days. Six hundred French troops marched out to acknowledge defeat, past half that number of healthy British. Formally, it meant that the Corsican campaign had been a victory – although, as Nelson complained to his wife and others, his own crucial part in it had not been acknowledged in despatches. As always, he craved glory and acclaim, and he felt betrayed.

He swallowed his pride and followed his orders, which now told him to seize Genoa for use as a base from which to harry the French as they fought their way down Italy towards Naples and Rome. Nelson made a rapid conquest here, and his vanity was soothed by the warmth of his reception by the local worthies. Meanwhile, the *Agamemnon* was in urgent need of repairs, which she received at Leghorn, and many of her crew were taken to hospitals. The fear was that France, which had enjoyed many land victories that year, was planning to retake Corsica.

By Christmas, the *Agamemnon* was seaworthy again. She sailed for Toulon to join Admiral Holtham, who had replaced Lord Hood when the latter returned to London to recover from illness. Here the British ships maintained a successful blockade. Nelson's spirits were high, until they were struck by storms of a strength he had never previously experienced. The *Agamemnon* rode the turbulent waters in style, but the crew did not. Nelson wrote to Hood:

Poor *Agamemnon* wants almost a new ship's

> company ... nor am I myself free from
> complaints. I have been so low with flux
> and fever this last cruise that I thought I
> shall hardly get over it.

He was snapped out of his low mood when word came that the French had sailed from Toulon and were headed for Corsica, as he had expected. Admiral Holtham had already engaged with the French, and the *Agamemnon* swiftly joined the attack. One of the largest French vessels, the *Ça Ira,* had accidentally collided with another ship and fallen behind. Nelson saw his chance, moved in on the straggler and bombarded her mercilessly until "the *Ça Ira* was a perfect wreck, her sails hanging in tatters, mizzen topmast, mizzen topsail and cross-jack yards shot away".

The *Ça Ira* was towed away from Nelson's attack by the *Censeur,* but Holtham opened fire on both of them, and the ships surrendered. The invasion of Corsica had been scotched; Nelson was eager to pursue the French ships as they fled, but Holtham persuaded him that they had done well enough. Nelson's blood was up; he was all for pursuing the fight, and wrote about his frustration to Fanny and others: "My disposition cannot bear tame and slow measures."

Fanny either did not note, or did not care, that Nelson was obviously craving her approval and admiration. Instead, her letters were full of fretting about his safety and health, not praise for his magnificence. He found this irritating as well as disappointing, and his affection for her waned by the letter. This may have been one of the reasons why he ended the year by having an affair with an opera singer, Adelaide Correglia, in Genoa. Some officers felt that their usually puritanical leader was making something of a fool of himself. But the affair was short-lived.

Nelson's career fortunes greatly improved early in 1796, when the Admiralty appointed Admiral Sir John Jervis as Hood's successor in the Mediterranean. Jervis and Nelson took to each other at once. Almost immediately, Jervis made him a commodore. (Jervis had tried to have Nelson promoted to rear-admiral, but had received no reply.) From this point on, the two men treated each other as equals.

It was just as well that these gifted men were of one mind, because the war was going badly for the British. Brigadier-general Napoleon seemed to be winning everywhere: he took Leghorn, and his advances in Italy seemed so unbeatable that the Spanish decided to change sides. From now on, the British were greatly outnumbered by the combined French and Spanish fleets. The Admiralty scented imminent defeat, and ordered that the Mediterranean be abandoned as swiftly as possible. Nelson was ordered to oversee the evacuation of Bastia, and then of Elba.

He had barely completed his tasks when he and his men encountered the Spanish. Nelson considered that he had two main options: he could search for Jervis and join him in battle, or he could sail to the West Indies to warn of the possibility of Spanish attack. He chose the former. When the friends were reunited aboard the *Victory*, Jervis explained that the Spanish were probably planning to take Cádiz. He also told him: "A victory is very essential to England at the moment."

This was an understatement. All of Continental Europe was now under the sway of France; the war had brought England to the brink of financial collapse; and there were rumours of mutiny in the lower ranks of the Royal Navy.

Cometh the hour, cometh the man.

The following action showed Nelson at his most fearless, and at his most insubordinate. As more than one historian has emphasised, no other naval officer of his rank had ever taken such a potentially disastrous risk, and perhaps none has since. Had his action failed, he would have faced a court-martial, and almost certainly been found guilty. He would have been ruined, and history would have largely forgotten him.

Nelson's sin? To "break the line", transgressing against a rule of combat that the Navy held sacred. From his perspective on the *Captain*, which was the last ship but two in the British fleet, Nelson could see that the leading British vessels were bound to arrive too late to keep the gap in the enemy's line open. So he ordered his crew to turn the *Captain* out of the line, initially sailing away from the enemy – a manoeuvre that could easily have been read as cowardice. But then he swung back, and aimed his ship directly at the rapidly closing gap, and engaged with no fewer than seven Spanish vessels.

He did not fight alone for long. Three more British ships soon joined him – the *Culloden*, captained by his friend Thomas Troubridge; the *Blenheim*, captained by Thomas Frederick; and the *Excellent*, which Cuthbert Collingwood commanded.

Nelson's courage in this battle was exceptional, even by his own standards. First, he drove the *Captain* right up against two of the largest Spanish vessels. As soon as the enemy was near enough, he jumped on board the enemy's deck, followed by his own sailors. The hand-to-hand fighting was bloody, and many on both sides incurred grave wounds – but the Spanish ship was soon taken.

Nelson and his men then boarded the second ship, and

fought with such ferocity that it, too, was soon captured. It was a short, bloody battle; in all, seventy-three British sailors were killed. But it was a decisive victory. Four Spanish ships were taken as prizes, two of them by the *Captain*. The gigantic *Santísima Trinidad* took a terrible battering, and was completely dismasted; only the arrival of escort ships saved her from being taken.

Despite his triumph, Nelson remained anxious that his commander-in-chief would condemn him for his reckless disregard for orders. He crossed over to the *Victory* as night was falling, fearing that Jervis would greet him with rage. Instead, as Nelson wrote:

> The Admiral received me on the quarter-deck, and having embraced me, said he could not sufficiently thank me, and used every kind expression which could not fail to make me happy.

News of the victory was warmly received back in England, and Jervis was handsomely rewarded by being made Earl of St Vincent. Nelson had become the hero of Britain, properly famous for the first time – though not as universally famous as he was to become over the next few years. He enjoyed it to the full, and sent Fanny a transcription of a new popular ballad that made much of the coincidence that the battle had been won on Valentine's Day:

> This hero brave, old England's boast
> grappled two ships along,
> forced them to strike on their own coast
> and lasting laurels won.
> Long will this day in history shine:

"Give me," the fair sex say,
"a Nelson for my Valentine
on this auspicious day."

Nelson also had his full reward of formal honours. Just a week after the battle, he was promoted to Rear-Admiral – to be exact, "Rear-Admiral of the Blue", the British fleet being divided into Red, White and Blue squadrons. At the age of thirty-eight, he was now the youngest admiral in the Navy. He was also made Knight of the Bath. For the next few years, until he achieved even higher honours, he would be Sir Horatio Nelson.

These were substantial laurels, but it was against everything in Nelson's character to rest upon them. He was put in command of the *Theseus* and given a small fleet of his own, with orders to patrol the waters close to the port of Cádiz, where the Spanish fleet was anchored, so as to prevent their ships from leaving the harbour.

On 3 July, he ordered that the town be bombarded. His plan was to provoke the Spanish into battle before their reinforcements could arrive. Nelson himself would go into action on a ten-oar barge, its small crew armed with pistols, pikes and cutlasses. This was another breach of the rulebook by him; he should really have stayed on his ship and controlled the actions from there. As night fell, the *Thunderer* shot mortar bombs high into the air, from where they rained down on the city. Nelson stood in the rear of his barge, enjoying the fireworks.

The Spanish came out to fight. The captain of one of their gunboats, Don Miguel Tyrason, identified Nelson as being in command of the barge, and sailed hard at it. The Spanish, who outnumbered the British two to one, boarded Nelson's barge brandishing swords, and the hand-to-hand fighting was ferocious. Nelson himself managed to fend off a blow that would almost certainly have been lethal; he was then saved from further deadly blows by the ship's corporal, John Sykes, who had been conspicuous for bravery at Cape St Vincent. One of the British sailors left a vivid account:

> John Sykes was close to Nelson on his left hand and he seemed more concerned with the Admiral's life than his own: he hardly ever struck a blow but to save his gallant officer. Twice he parried blows that must have been fatal to Nelson ... It was cut, thrust, fire and no load again – we had no time for that. The Spaniards fought like devils and seemed to resolve to win from the Admiral the laurels of his former victory: they appeared to know him and directed their particular attack towards the officers.
>
> Twice Sykes saved him; and now he saw a blow descending that would have severed the head of Nelson. In that second of thought that a cool man possesses, Sykes saw that he could not ward the blow with his cutlass ... He saw the danger; that moment expired and Nelson would have been a corpse: but Sykes saved him – he interposed his own hand! We all saw it ... and we gave in revenge one cheer and one tremendous rally.

Nelson was moved: "Sykes," he said, "I cannot forget this." Soon, eighteen Spanish sailors lay dead on the barge; the British boarded their gunboat, and took it.

Noting his triumph, the Admiralty told Nelson to apply his skills in an attack on the island of Tenerife – to be exact, on its main port, Santa Cruz, where ships laden with treasure from the New World would call, and might be taken. St Vincent was told that a tempting new target, a bullion ship from Manila named *El Principe de Asturias*, was at anchor there. On 14 July, he duly ordered Nelson to lead a squadron of four ships to Tenerife and seize both the ship and the port. Nelson set out the following day. The journey took six days.

The main plan was to send 1,000 marines in frigates, to be landed to the east of Santa Cruz before dawn under the command of Troubridge, and to stage a surprise attack as day broke. But, to the dismay of the British, the currents undid this scheme: the waters drove them back out to sea and threatened to scatter them. Troubridge saw that the crucial element of surprise had been lost, and ordered the frigates to retreat and join the big ships.

Nelson was determined to go ahead with the action, even though the crews of the small boats were now exhausted after long hours at the oars. The big ships opened fire at the shore, and the small boats made again for shore under cover of this bombardment. This time they made it to land – but the feat was short-lived. Troubridge soon realised that he had neither the strength nor the numbers to make a frontal assault, and at dusk he ordered another retreat to sea. A strong gale blew up, and the sailors struggled to keep control of the vessels.

On the next day, 24 July, with the gale still raging, Nelson summoned his captains to a conference on board the *Theseus*. To their surprise, he told them that he intended to make a direct assault on Santa Cruz that night. It seemed reckless, but Nelson had heard a report that the Spanish forces – just 300 regular soldiers and a force of peasant conscripts who were hopelessly inadequate in battle – were enfeebled and demoralised.

The action began at 10.30 PM. The officers and men went down into their various barges, which were loosely roped together, and set off across two miles of turbulent water. Their orders were to scale the walls of the castle (San Cristóbal), storm it, and the take the city. The Spanish knew they were coming, and their sentries were posted and wide awake. Shortly after 1.00 AM, they had their first sight of the British. The gunfire began; it was, as a British lieutenant put it, "truly warm!".

Nelson was one of the first ashore, brandishing a fighting sword that had been given to him by Captain Suckling. Almost immediately, he reeled, staggered, and crawled his way back to the boat, his right arm pumping blood from a shot wound. He fell, saying, "I am a dead man." Nelson's stepson, Josiah Nisbet, thought quickly and tore the black silk stocking from around his neck to use as a tourniquet. He saw that Nelson was in urgent need of a surgeon, and ordered the boat's crew to pull away from the shore and take him back to one of the ships. The first one they encountered was Thomas Fremantle's command, the *Seahorse*, but Nelson stubbornly insisted that he be taken further on to his own ship, *Theseus*. Nisbet pleaded with him, saying that he was in imminent danger of dying. Nelson was adamant:

> Then I will die. I would rather suffer death than alarm Mrs Fremantle by her seeing

me in this state when I can give her no
tidings of her husband.

Eventually, they reached the *Theseus*. A young midshipman saw Nelson, "his right arm dangling by his side while
with his left he jumped up the ship's side and, with a
spirit that astonished everyone, told the surgeon to get his
instruments ready, for he knew that he must lose his arm,
and the sooner it was off the better". Thomas Eshelby, the
surgeon, saw that Nelson's self-diagnosis was correct, and
he began the amputation without pausing to dose Nelson
with opium. It was agonising, but mercifully brief. The
limb, on Nelson's orders, was thrown overboard. (Like
many patients who undergo an amputation, Nelson often
sensed his missing arm as a 'phantom limb', and chose to
regard the experience as concrete proof of the existence of
an immortal soul.)

Meanwhile, on shore, the British were being met with
massive resistance. Not only had the intelligence report
about the poor morale of the Spanish been entirely wrong;
they had just been joined by reinforcements from all over
the island, so that the garrison was manned by approx-
imately 8,000 troops as well as a French artillery unit
commanding forty field guns. They rained fire down on
the British, cutting the invasion force to pieces.

Despite the heavy casualties, the British continued
to fight. They made their way through the streets under
heavy sniper fire; when they reached squares, bigger guns
fired at them. By dawn, they raised a flag of parley; but it
was a bluff. The Spanish commander, Lieutenant-General
Antonio Gutiérrez, rightly ignored it. Troubridge, now
leading some 340 exhausted men, tried again. Again, his
bluff was called. The spirits of the British rallied when they

saw what they took to be a relief party, but this as in fact no more than the survivors of the initial assault, finally wading ashore.

Troubridge made a final offer of parley, this one more sincere, but Gutiérrez was adamant. There was no alternative but to seek terms of surrender, offering to retreat provided they were treated with full military honours. Gutiérrez found this acceptable, and the British troops duly fell in, emptied their muskets by firing them into the sea, and then handed over all their weapons. At first, the Spanish victors treated them with courtesy; then they began to jeer and taunt the defeated. The officers were invited to dine with Gutiérrez, and accepted, though they remained almost mute with grief. One hundred and fifty-three men had been shot or drowned, and many received wounds from which they soon died.

Gutiérrez proved as magnanimous in victory as he had been ferocious in combat. He freely allowed the British to take their wounded from the hospital back to their ships, and he and Nelson exchanged lavish gifts, including a barrel of English ale and two demijohns of the best Canary wine. When the body of the last British officer had been committed to the waves, Nelson's fleet sailed away. He had suffered a terrible defeat – the worst of his life – in part due to his misguided contempt for the Spanish, whose forces he had defeated with such flair in the recent past.

Only on very rare occasions did Nelson give in to despair, and this was one of them. A few days later, writing for the first time with his left hand, he wrote to St Vincent in the most despondent terms:

> I am become a burthen to my friends and
> useless to my country. When I leave your

command **I** become dead to the world; I
go hence and am no more seen. I hope you
will give me a frigate to convey the remains
of my carcass to England.

A left-handed admiral will never again be
considered as useful, therefore the sooner
I get to a very humble cottage the better
and make room for a better man to serve
the state.

The gloom was sincere, but it lifted as Nelson returned to England and discovered that he was being lauded on all sides. In a season of ominous news for Britain – Napoleon had defeated the Austrians and annexed northern Italy, and sailors in the Royal Navy had committed the unthinkable crime of mutiny – the nation was in sore need of a hero. Nelson fit the bill. Disastrous as the failed invasion of Santa Cruz had been, it was a dark spot that was outshone by his glorious victories at Cádiz and Cape St Vincent.

Although Fanny was not given to demonstrations of affection, she cared for Nelson with a tenderness that soothed his mind as well as his broken body. She was fastidious, washing and re-dressing his septic wound every day and giving him doses of laudanum. He was in chronic pain until, in November, the infected ligatures from surgery finally came free, and he began to heal.

Nelson's spirits were raised by the rewards heaped on him. The government gave him a pension of £1,000 a year, and, once he was well enough, the City of London gave him the Freedom of the City, and King George III invited him to court. In Norwich, the museum displayed the swords he had taken from the Spanish. He bought a home of decent size, "Roundwood", in the countryside near the East Anglian town of Ipswich. There Fanny could finally act the lady of the house to her heart's content. When his pain permitted, he and Fanny would socialise with grand folk. One of them, Lady Spencer, the wife of the new First Lord of the Admiralty, recorded a sharp impression of how the newly famous Nelson appeared at this time:

> The first time I saw him was in the drawing-room of the Admiralty, and a most uncouth creature I thought him. He had just returned from Tenerife, after having lost his arm. He looked so sickly that it was painful to see him, and his general appearance was that of an idiot, so much so that, when he spoke and his wonderful mind broke forth, it was a sort of surprise that riveted my whole attention.

The better he felt, the more he burned to be back at sea, in pursuit of the French. In the spring of 1798, the Admiralty finally agreed to allow him back in active service. He was originally supposed to have been given command of the new *Foudroyant*, but her construction was not yet complete, so he was given the *Vanguard*, of seventy-four guns. He set sail on 29 March, and by May 4 he was back in the Mediterranean at the head of three men-of-war, four frigates and a sloop.

His mission was to make a voyage of reconnaissance, and to determine what Napoleon's overall strategy in the Mediterranean might be. Throughout the spring, London had been hearing reports of a giant fleet being massed at Toulon under Napoleon himself, now commander of the French military. That he was planning a major action was obvious, but what was his target? Portugal – Britain's ally at the time? Ireland, where there was an armed revolt against British rule? The Kingdom of Naples? Constantinople?

On 17 May, Nelson's frigate, the *Terpsichore*, took a French corvette. When its crew were interrogated, they revealed that Napoleon had prepared fifteen ships of the line, on which 12,000 troops had already been embarked. The commander of the enemy fleet was Vice-Admiral François-Paul Brueys, on board the gigantic ship *Orient*, of 120 guns. But the captives could not give any clue as to Napoleon's master plan.

Nelson's fleet watched and waited. Then, disaster struck: a fierce gale suddenly burst upon the British. The *Vanguard* was hit hard. One by one, he main-topmast, the mizzen and the foremast all cracked and went overboard. Sails and masts and rigging dragged the ship down, and until the crew had managed to hack the tangles free, she was in peril of going down or crashing on the rocks. Worse news soon followed: the same winds that had almost destroyed Nelson's fleet had carried the French, unseen, out of Toulon and out of sight.

In a letter to his wife dated 24 May, Nelson wrote:

> I ought not to call what has happened to the *Vanguard* by the cold name of accident: I believe firmly that it was the Almighty's goodness, to check my consummate vanity. I hope it has made me a better officer, as I feel confident it has made me a better man. Figure to yourself, on Sunday evening, at

sunset, a vain man walking in his cabin, with a squadron around him, who looked up to their chief to lead them to glory, and in whom their chief placed the firmest reliance that that proudest ships of equal numbers belonging to France would have lowered their flags; figure to yourself, on Monday morning, when the sun rose, this proud man, his ship dismasted, his fleet dispersed, and himself in such tress that the meanest frigate out of France would have been an unwelcome guest.

Nelson took shelter in a Sardinian port and set about repairing his damaged ship. Thanks to the exceptional skill of the carpenter in charge, this considerable task took only five days; and yet, by the time the *Vanguard* was seaworthy again, the French fleet, with Napoleon, was already well on its way to its still-mysterious destination. They had an advantage on Nelson of eighteen days; it was not until June 7 that he could begin his pursuit, now reinforced by eleven ships of the line that had been sent from Gibraltar on Admiralty orders, including *Goliath*, *Minotaur*, *Defence*, *Bellepheron*, *Majestic*, *Zealous*, *Swiftsure*, *Theseus* and *Audacious*.

It was, as one maritime historian put it, "perhaps the finest squadron of its size ever assembled in the age of sail". There was just one flaw – Nelson lacked enough frigates, the swift sailing 'eyes' of a fleet. There was no doubt that his forces were strong enough to attack the French, but where exactly were they? Nelson wrote to Hamilton: "My distress for frigates is extreme … I cannot help myself, and no one will help me. But, thank God, I am not apt to feel difficulties."

Intelligence reached them that merchant ships had seen the French sailing past Corsica towards Italy. It suggested that they were planning an attack on Naples and Sicily, or perhaps Malta. When the British reached Naples, Nelson remained aboard ship and sent Troubridge and Thomas Hardy to confer with Sir William Hamilton. They found that the city was in dread of a French attack and dared not lend Nelson the frigates he so badly needed, for fear of offending. But the Prime Minister was willing to sign an order to allow Sicily to provide Nelson's men with the food and water, of which they were now in desperate need.

Nelson set course for Malta, but the news reached him that the island had just fallen to the French, on 15 July. The other places where he might perhaps find Napoleon were Corfu – controlled by the Venetians, allies of France – or Egypt. He called his four main captains to join him on the *Vanguard* to work out their best course of action. After due reflection, he decided to go with a hunch that he had been considering for weeks: that Napoleon's target must be Egypt.

He decided on the latter course. At one point during the race to Egypt, the British fleet drew so close to the French that Brueys could actually hear their signal guns. He panicked; but Napoleon stayed calm.

Chapter Four

Egypt, Naples, Sicily, 1798–99

The Battle of the Nile
Moving at top speed, the British actually reached Egypt before the enemy. They found Alexandria in a state of war – but the antagonists were Turkish. There were no French in sight. Nelson requested permission to take on water and food, but the Turks refused him. He was obliged to make a strategic retreat to Sicily, where each ship took on some 250 tons of fresh water, and food of the finest quality available. The latter was not an indulgence: Nelson was well aware of how illness could afflict sailors who were not properly fed, and took justifiable pride that so far he had "not one sick man" in the whole squadron. He also took the opportunity to train his officers and men up to the highest levels – fire drills, gun practice and detailed briefings about his strategy for the fight ahead. Meanwhile, Napoleon had landed unopposed at Fort Marabout in Alexandria.

Eventually, the British received intelligence that the

French were now in the city: Nelson had guessed correctly, and simply been too prompt. By 1 August, his ships once again entered the waters off Alexandria's harbour – the harbour itself being too silted for their use. From this vantage point, they could see the French fleet, spread out from Aboukir Bay to the Rosetta mouth of the Nile. One of Nelson's officers, Captain Edward Berry, wrote:

> The utmost joy seemed to animate every breast on board the squadron at the sight of the Enemy, and the pleasure which the Admiral himself felt was perhaps more heightened than that of any other man, as he now had a certainty by which he could regulate his future operations.

Indeed, Nelson, always hungry for distinction, said to his brother officers on the eve of battle: "Before this time tomorrow, I shall have gained a peerage or Westminster Abbey."

He determined to fight at once, and sent a series of signals: twice to prepare for action, and then, at 5.40 PM, to prepare for close action. Just forty minutes later, *Goliath*, captained by Thomas Foley – an officer who rivalled Nelson for audacity and decisiveness – steered for the anchor-cable of the French van-ship *Guerrier*, shot past her and then into the waters behind her. *Zealous* and *Theseus* followed on her stern, while *Orion* and *Audacious* sailed directly through the enemy line. Within just twelve minutes, *Guerrier* had been dismasted. Nelson, now anchored on the seaboard side of Brueys, ordered the remaining ships to make a direct attack on the French centre. He also ordered the gunners of *Vanguard* to commence a bombardment of *Spartiate*. He took a serious wound during this action – a piece of iron shot hit his forehead, and the flow of blood over his eyes rendered him temporarily blind. "I am killed!" he shouted. "Remember me to my wife!" Men carried him below to the surgeon, Michael Jefferson, but when he saw that Jefferson was already busy with sailors who had even more dangerous wounds, Nelson said: "No, I will take my turn with my brave fellows." Later, he confessed that he had been sure he was about to die.

Meanwhile, *Spartiate* surrendered after two hours of resistance. She was joined by *Guerrier, Conquérant, Aquilon* and *Peuple Souverain*. Other ships and their captains put up an almost suicidal resistance. The captain of the *Tonnant*, Aristide Aubert Dupetit Thouars, was so badly wounded in both legs and one arm that he ordered his men to bring a tub of bran and put his shattered body in it. He urged them to fight on, as he gradually bled to death.

The most spectacular event of the night-time battle was the destruction of the *Orient*, the largest and grandest ship in the French fleet. Brueys, both its captain and the commander-in-chief of the operation, was also seriously wounded, taking one shot in the head and two in the body, until a final shot cut him in two. The *Orient* was loaded with exceptional treasure – half a million pounds' worth of gold, three tons of precious plate, and a collection of silver statues. She also carried a cargo of explosive chemicals. When, at about 9.00 PM, she caught fire, it became obvious that she was about to explode. In an act of chivalry not uncommon during that era of warfare, the injured Nelson gave the order that as many French lives as possible should be saved.

Vanguard's one useable small boat was sent across as

the enemy ship blazed. It picked up seventy French sailors who had thrown themselves into the sea. At 10.00 PM, the *Orient* exploded. The noise was so terrible that many sailors aboard other vessels were sure it must have been their own ships that had blown up. Fifteen miles away, in Alexandria, the noise was still loud enough to make the troops jump. Then came a huge rain of debris over both sides.

Battle resumed, apart from a brief pause in which British and French alike gave in to sheer exhaustion, and carried on until 3.00 in the morning. The French ships took terrible damage: *Serieuse* was sunk, and *Artémise* set on fire by her own captain. By dawn, only two ships of the line (one of them, the *Guillaume Tell*, was captained by Nelson's future adversary at Trafalgar, Villeneuve) and two frigates cut their lines and fled. The British were in no condition to give chase, but it did not matter greatly. Their victory was, in effect, absolute.

Surveying Aboukir Bay on the morning of 2 August 1798, Nelson gazed at what was left of the French fleet and reflected that "[v]ictory is not a name strong enough for such a scene". Historians have tended to agree with his sentiment: "No British victory at sea," wrote one, "had ever been so complete, and obtained without the loss of a single ship." French losses were estimated at 5,225 men either killed, drowned, burned, or captured – six times the number of British casualties.

Nelson made sure the whole world knew of his triumph. Among the messengers he despatched was a young lieutenant who brought the glorious news to British interests in India and others that had been dreading Napoleon's plans to extend France's dominion east of Suez. The East India Company voted Nelson a present of £10,000 – an extraordinary sum. The *Mutine*, a French ship captured at

Santa Cruz and recommissioned by the British, brought the word to Naples and thence all of Europe. The Queen of Naples fainted with relief and bliss. So did Emma Hamilton, who shortly afterwards wrote:

> I am delirious with joy, and assure you that I have a fever caused by agitation and pleasure. Good God what a victory! Never has there been anything quite so glorious, so complete!

> ... I fainted when I heard the joyful news, and fell on my side, and am hurt, but what of that ... I should feel it a glory to die in such a cause. No, I would not like to die until I see and embrace the *Victor of the Nile* ... Sir William is ten years younger since the happy news ... My dress from head to foot is *alla Nelson*. Even my shawl is in Blue with gold anchors all over. My ear-rings are Nelson's anchors; in short, we are all be-Nelsoned ...

Countless voices echoed her fervour. The British press exploded with praise for England's hero, and the makers of souvenirs – prints, mugs, plates, handkerchiefs – produced a torrent of Nelsonian merchandise. Quite literally overnight, Nelson had become the most famous Englishman in the world, more famous even than his Prime Minister and King.

Nelson was, to be sure, hugely gratified when he learned of this popular frenzy, but in the meantime the *Vanguard* was in urgent need of repairs. He sailed for Naples, and arrived there on 22 September.

Naples and Sicily

It was not only repairs he had in mind. Nelson had gradually become convinced that King Ferdinand IV of Naples was a loyal and potentially useful ally of Britain, and that the two most important British representatives in the kingdom, Sir William Hamilton and Sir John Acton (the prime minister of Naples), were both resourceful and efficient. And Hamilton, as Nelson soon learned, admired him almost as much as Lady Hamilton did. Thrilled at the "hawk-like" decisiveness of Nelson's tactics in the recent campaign, Hamilton enthused:

> That is the way to do business ... How proud I am of feeling myself an Englishman at this moment. Great Britain alone has truly faced the enemy in support of the good cause, and Nelson is the greatest hero of Great Britain.

During this same period of residence, Nelson, often noted for his strict adherence to the chivalric conduct of war and his frequent acts of humanity, meted out bloody and merciless punishment to the Neapolitan rebels who briefly took control of the city – an act that his harshest critics regard as unforgiveable treachery.

Emma and William

In 1799, Nelson began his famous affair with Emma Hamilton – today, generally regarded as one of the greatest love stories in British history, but in their own day, and for much of the nineteenth century, a major public scandal and an embarrassment. The affair was either denied or simply ignored by most of Nelson's biographers. Southey

perceptibly squirms when he describes Nelson's "infatuated attachment for Lady Hamilton, which totally weaned
his affections from his wife":

> Farther than this, there is no reason
> to believe that this most unfortunate
> attachment was criminal; – but this was
> criminality enough, and it brought with it
> its punishment.

Was anyone ever truly persuaded by such words?

From that year until the death of the English diplomat in 1803, Horatio, Emma and William were united
in a *ménage à trois* rare both in its celebrity and apparent
happiness. All three participants were remarkable each in
their own way. They referred to themselves by the Latin
phrase *tria juncta in uno* – "three joined in one" – which
was the motto of the Order of the Bath, to which both
Horatio and William belonged.

Sir William was sixty-eight at the time. A tall, slender,
serious-looking gentleman distinguished both in appearance and reality, he was by temperament a scholar and
scientist, and by passion a collector and connoisseur, especially of classical antiquities. His circumstances, however,
had forced him into a life of public service. As the younger
son of a younger son he had little money of his own, but
had put that right in 1758 when he married a young heir-
ess, who brought to the marriage an estate in Wales worth
some £8,000 a year. Six years later he joined the diplomatic service and accepted a posting to Naples, where the
warm climate and fresh sea breezes would be good for the
fragile health of his bride. She was happy enough here,
and seems to have doted on William, but succumbed to

illness in 1782. The following year, William brought her remains back to Britain for burial. There he had a fateful meeting with a strikingly beautiful young woman who, at the time, was calling herself "Emma Hart". She was the mistress of his nephew; soon she would be the second Lady Hamilton.

Emma Hart, *née* Amy Lyon, was born in 1765 to an illiterate blacksmith and his wife in the Wirral Peninsula, Cheshire. Her home village was one of the most impoverished in England – little more than a gathering of filthy hovels, home mainly to the miners who worked in a nearby pit. Her rapid and triumphal rise is quite remarkable – in its way, quite as much an accomplishment as Horatio Nelson's rise to glory. By the age of twelve she had found a place as an under-housemaid for a Welsh surgeon; a year or so later she moved to London and became a maidservant, took to modelling and then, it is conjectured, may have worked as a prostitute. She was taken up as mistress to a young baronet, who abandoned her when she became pregnant.

She was next kept by the Hon. Charles Greville, second son of the Earl of Warwick and nephew to Sir William. When Greville decided that he, too, wished to marry for money, he pressed her on William, who was delighted by the arrangement. Though Emma was heartbroken by Greville's rejection, she was a pragmatist and set about making herself both charming and useful to Sir William. Soon the older man was smitten, and in 1791 he made her his wife. But she also charmed the local royals, too. For eight years before Nelson pulled in to dock, she enjoyed great success as a society hostess of international reputation, and a favourite of the Neapolitan court – especially of the queen, who became an intimate friend.

The court of Naples took its tone from King Ferdinand

IV, who was slow-witted, infantile, gluttonous, cowardly, vindictive, and so gross in his personal habits – such as ritual acts of public defecation – that he disgusted all but the coarsest of his courtiers. Sir William, fastidious to a fault, found his company close to unbearable, but he knew his duty and he did it without open complaint. Hard as it may be to credit, Ferdinand was considered by his father, Charles III of Spain, a better candidate for the monarchy than his two older brothers. The oldest one was quite insane, and had to be forcibly restrained from molesting any woman who came near him; the second was an idiot. Ferdinand, being merely stupid and obnoxious, was the best of the bunch.

Curiously, Ferdinand was sincerely loved by the Neapolitan populace, as he shared most of their favourite pastimes: hunting (more exactly, mass slaughter of animals – he would have his servants herd game towards him and blast away, killing them all), sailing, and fishing, at which he was genuinely talented. He enjoyed dressing up as a common fisherman, selling his catch in the markets and haggling fiercely over the price in the local dialect.

His wife, Maria Carolina, was a far superior creature. Born in 1752, this daughter of an empress and sister to the guillotined Marie Antoinette was left with a fear and loathing of all forms of radicalism in general, and the French kind in particular. She was married off to Ferdinand at the age of sixteen – he was just a year older – and had to submit frequently to his sexual demands, however little she relished them. She bore him no fewer than eighteen children, of whom eight survived.

Despite her many labours, Maria Carolina was able to apply her considerable intelligence to affairs of state; by about 1775, she was, in effect, the true ruler of Naples,

Ferdinand being bored by the whole business; he seems to have been frightened by her rages on the rare occasions when he tried to resist her. Nelson found her impressive, as well he might. She had true regal manners – Nelson loved a monarch – as well as a keen grasp of European politics, a will of iron and a hatred of the French that, if anything, exceeded his own.

When Nelson arrived in Naples after an absence of five years, both Emma and Sir William were shocked at the sight of their old friend. In addition to the loss of his arm and eye, the bloody head wound he had taken at Aboukir Bay was still far from adequately healed, and he suffered from constant headaches. He had also been feverish on the journey from Egypt to Naples, and the combination of anxiety and pain he had been enduring rendered him haggard and weak. For his first weeks in Naples he was a recovering invalid, yet the demands of his official and private correspondence were so unrelenting that he could not allow himself a proper period of rest.

Nor could he refuse to take part in the many lavish celebrations that were mounted in his honour, of which the grandest was a party celebrating his fortieth birthday on 29 September. There were some 1,800 guests, each of them wearing buttons or ribbons with the inscription *H. N. Glorious 1ˢᵗ of August*. When the national anthem was sung, it contained a new and topical verse:

> Join we great Nelson's name
> First on the roll of fame
> Him let us sing!
>
> Spread we his fame around,
> Honour of British ground,

Who made Nile's shores resound.
God save the King!

Gifts and honours poured in from Britain and around the world: a gold medal from George III; a peerage – "Baron Nelson of the Nile and Burnham Thorpe"; a pension of £2,000 *per annum* from Parliament; a sword from the City of London; a diamond *çelenk* [a dramatic decoration with thirteen diamonds representing the ships taken in battle] from the Ottoman Sultan; a diamond box from the Tsar of Russia; and a gold-headed cane from the Ionian island of Zakynthos, whose inhabitants believed that Nelson's victory had liberated them from French tyranny.

His oddest gift was from Admiral Benjamin Hallowell of the *HMS Swiftsure*, who sent him a coffin made from part of the *Orient*'s main-mast, "that, when you are tired of Life, you may be buried in one of your own Trophies". Other men might have been angered or dismayed, but Nelson relished the macabre present so much that he had it set up in his cabin behind his dinner chair, until he was begged to have it stowed away below. He swore that it was his intent that no one else's remains should be placed in it, and a few years later, at Trafalgar, was able to keep his word.

Despite his resounding victory, Naples and other parts of Italy were still being menaced by the French armies; in fact, only Pope Pius VI and King Ferdinand still retained some degree of autonomy. Ferdinand was keen to strike the first blow with an attack on the French, and Nelson agreed with the sentiment – though he had his doubts about the effete and ill-disciplined Neapolitans' chance of victory. "The miserable conduct of [Ferdinand's] court," he wrote, "is not likely to cool my irritable temper … It is a country of fiddlers and poets, whores and scoundrels."

In fact, Naples's campaign against the French began in promising fashion. Under the command of the Austrian Karl Mack von Leiberich, its army advanced on the enemy in five columns, while Nelson, with 4,000 men, sailed north-west up the Italian coast to seize Leghorn and so cut French communications. Mack's forces met with minimal resistance in Rome, and soon had the city under near-complete control – but not for long. By early December, the French were back in control of the Eternal City, and pushed home their advantage by heading directly for Naples. Nelson's mood was grim: "If Mack is defeated, in fourteen days this country is lost, for the Holy Roman Emperor has not yet moved his army, and Naples has not the power of resisting the enemy." Subsequent days confirmed his worst predictions: Mack made a poor show of resistance, and his officers were singularly incompetent. Nelson growled that they had not lost much honour, "for God knows they had not much to lose – but they lost all they had".

By 18 December, Mack presented himself at court and said that it would be impossible to stop the advancing French forces. The only realistic option was for Nelson to help the royal family sail to Sicily. As Nelson felt some culpability for having encouraged Mack's ill-fated campaign, he agreed. By means of an underground tunnel that led from the castle to the shore, he conducted the king, queen and their large entourage aboard the *Vanguard*, along with about 2.5 million pounds' worth of treasure. They set sail on 23 December.

It was a horrific crossing, even for experienced sailors; for the passengers, it was hell. Within a day they had sailed into the most violent storm even Nelson had ever encountered. Most of the civilians were afflicted with terrible seasickness. Sir William, who was terrified of death by drowning, cradled a brace of pistols with which to blow off his head rather than experience the "guggle, guggle, guggle of salt water in his throat" should the ship go down. Emma was heroic in her actions as a self-appointed nurse, though her best efforts could not help the youngest royal child, who died on the second day at sea.

They finally escaped the storm and made a safe landing at Palermo on 26 December. The refugees stayed in Palermo for the rest of the winter, for the most part in poor spirits. Sir William was harrowed by the news that the ship on which he had loaded the finest items of his classical vase collection had been sunk on the way to England; almost nothing could be salvaged. Nelson was frequently depressed, and admitted feeling that he did not have much longer to live. The general mood sank lower still when the French army in Naples finally overcame the local resistance, and – with the keen participation of many from the middle classes and liberal aristocracy – established what became known as the Vesuvian or Parthenopean Republic. This was intolerable, and had to be resisted: for a few weeks, the main agent for resistance to the Jacobin alliance was one Cardinal Fabrizio Ruffo, a remarkably competent and multi-talented man who soon raised a force of about 300 men as a counter-revolutionary army, which was joined by various allies. They put down all opposition in Southern Italy with such ferocity that the campaign has often been described as a kind of White Terror.

There was more good news for the royals: the long-expected war between France and the Holy Roman Empire had finally broken out, Russian troops were on the march to Italy, and a British regiment had landed in Sicily to help with its defence. But there was also ominous news: a new

French fleet had entered the Mediterranean, probably – or so Nelson and his wards feared – to head for Alexandria, where they would turn loose the trapped French army and then both attack Sicily and rally to the side of the Parthenopean Republic in Naples.

On 5 June, British reinforcements arrived in Palermo, including a splendid new eighty-gun ship, the *Foudroyant* – to which Nelson at once transferred his flag from the *Vanguard*. With this powerful weapon now in his hands, Nelson thought he had the opportunity to wrest Naples from the hands of the rebels. It was not an easy decision for him: his first duty was not to restore the Bourbon monarchy, but to keep his ships at the ready to attack the French wherever they went in the Mediterranean, especially if they made the feared attempt on Egypt. After some inconclusive manoeuvrings on both sides, Nelson was finally given a direct order by King Ferdinand and Queen Maria Carolina to retake Naples.

Full of misgivings, Nelson reluctantly decided to obey the order. What followed was both complex and distressing. For Nelson's detractors, it provides evidence of his wickedness; for many of his admirers, it was a rare, possibly unique lapse from his usual high ethical standards in the conduct of war. Few regard it as inconsequential.

Broadly, the incident concerns the treatment of a defeated enemy. While Nelson's fleet (of seventeen ships) was coming close to Naples, it received intelligence that Ruffo had granted the rebels an armistice of twenty-one days, at the end of which they were to surrender their last two outposts – the castles of dell'Ovo and Nuovo – after which they were to be transported to France if their forces had not been relieved by the Combined Fleet.

Nelson was not happy with this proposal. He insisted

that the French soldiers should be given just two hours to evacuate, then be forcibly escorted back to France, while the local Jacobins must beg mercy from their restored king. He sailed into the Bay of Naples on 24 June, determined to enforce this policy. Taken by surprise, the town's royalists were delighted, while the rebels quickly hoisted white flags of surrender. Almost immediately, both the French and the Jacobins signed a formal agreement of capitulation. But when Nelson learned the terms of their surrender, he was furious at the generosity of its terms to the "traitors", which included agreements that the Neapolitans should retain all their property and not in any way be molested. It was, in effect, a complete pardon, and Nelson thought it disgraceful.

He sent lieutenants to Ruffo to argue his objections, and the arguments became heated. Eventually, they asked Ruffo whether or not he would support Nelson should the admiral decide to take arms against the rebels. Ruffo flatly refused. He was taken on board the *Foudroyant* to state his case in person, and, once again, tempers were lost. Gradually, though, Nelson decided that although he would proceed with military action against the rebels, he would slightly moderate the terms of war. Now, the Jacobins would be allowed to make an orderly retreat and flee by sea. Nelson ordered attacks on rebel strongholds in the three castles (Castel Sant'Elmo included), which were successful. The defeated men, who had signed their capitulation to Ruffo in the confident belief that they would be given safe passage to quit the town, were seized and imprisoned.

Unfortunately for the rebels, Nelson had been instructed by Queen Maria Carolina to "treat Naples as if it were a rebellious Irish town": he must consider no humane compromises, and he should make an example of the rebel leaders. Ruffo had exceeded his brief (this was true enough), and the terms offered in his armistice need not be respected. At first, Nelson did little more than tell the leaders of the Republic that they should plead humbly for the clemency of the king when he came ashore. But then King Ferdinand arrived, and with him came horror.

The trials and executions that followed have been described as, at best, judicial murders. At worst, they were a form of massacre. One of the first victims was the highly distinguished Admiral Prince Francesco Caracciolo, formerly a loyal servant of the Kingdom, who had cast his lot in with the new Republic. Caracciolo was seized, treated to a show trial (no witnesses, no counsel), condemned, and hanged from the yardarm – a calculated rebuke to his wish to be given an end more suitable for a nobleman. His body was cut down, and fell into the water. A little later, the superstitious Ferdinand was terrified when he saw the floating corpse bobbing towards him on the waves. People joked that Caracciolo had come back to beg forgiveness; but Ferdinand was not comforted.

Meanwhile, hundreds of rebels slowly awaited their own sham trials and inevitable executions while crammed into filthy Neapolitan prisons. When news of Nelson's actions spread throughout Europe, the Hero suddenly became a villain in the eyes of civilised opinion. It was felt that Nelson had been a willing dupe of Ferdinand, and had used his power to carry out a bloody and vindictive revenge. Increasingly, the executed and imprisoned were seen as martyrs, and the Royal Navy as the tool of a petty tyrant. Even Southey, Nelson's first biographer – a man who all but worshipped his subject – felt that Naples was the one great blot on his life:

... the garrisons, taken out of the castles,
under pretence of carrying the treaty into
effect, were delivered over as rebels to
the vengeance of the Sicilian court. - A
deplorable transaction! A stain upon the
memory of Nelson, and the honour of
England! To palliate it would be in vain;
to justify it would be wicked; there is no
alternative, for one who will not make
himself a participator in guilt, but to
record the disgraceful story with sorrow
and with shame.

Southey's conclusion is even more damning:

In expelling the French from Naples,
Nelson had, with characteristic zeal
and ability, discharged his duty; but he
deceived himself when he imagined that
he had seated Ferdinand firmly on his
throne, and that he had restored happiness
to millions. These objects might have been
accomplished if it had been possible to
inspire virtue and wisdom into a vicious
and infatuated court; and if Nelson's eyes
had not been, as it were spellbound by
that unhappy attachment [i.e. to Lady
Hamilton] which had now completely
mastered him, he would have seen things
as they were; and might, perhaps, have
awakened the Sicilian court to a sense of
their interest, if not their duty. That court
employed itself in a miserable round of folly

and festivity, while the prisons of Naples were filled with groans, and the scaffolds streamed with blood.

Yet there is no hint in Nelson's correspondence that he felt he had behaved anything other than properly. Not long after the events of Naples, he disobeyed orders from his superior, Baron Keith, because he judged them to be ill-advised. What he said of that act of insubordination applies just as well to his treatment of the rebels and French in Naples. In a letter to the Duke of Clarence, he explained:

> To serve the King, and to destroy the French, I consider as the great order of all, from which all little ones spring; and if one of these little ones militate against it (for, who can tell exactly at a distance?), I go back and obey the great order and object, to *down, down* with the damned French villains..

> Excuse my warmth; but my blood boils at the name of a Frenchman.

On 8 August, Nelson sailed back to Palermo with King Ferdinand, who lost no time in bestowing a fresh honour on the admiral – the Dukedom of Bronte. In addition to the title, which delighted Nelson so much that he eventually began to sign himself "Nelson & Bronte" or "Nelson Bronte", the estate was meant to bring him a revenue of about £3,000 a year.

Over the following year, Nelson took part in a number of marine battles; for one of them, on a trip to Malta, he was accompanied by Emma, who had found the experience of being under fire from a shore battery unexpectedly exhilarating. About a year later, Nelson reminisced fondly about the "days of ease and nights of pleasure" with which this sail ended. In other words, his affair with Emma had at last been consummated. From this point until his death, Horatio and Emma were lovers.

Chapter Five

Copenhagen, England and the War with France

The Passage Home and the Battle of Copenhagen
In June, Nelson received a letter from Lord Spencer, which – though couched in terms of the greatest solicitude – contained a tacit order he could scarcely refuse:

> It is by no means my wish or intention
> to call you away from service, but having
> observed that you have been under the
> necessity of quitting your station off Malta,
> on account of the state of your health,
> which I am persuaded you could not have
> thought of doing without such necessity,
> it appeared to me much more advisable
> for you to come home at once, than to be
> obliged to remain inactive at Palermo ...

And so on. The message was clear. *Come back to England*

at once. Nelson was ready to obey, but there were practical difficulties. Lord Keith said that he simply could not afford to part with the *Foudroyant.* He was not unreasonable, and offered Nelson his choice of troop ships for the voyage home. This would have been an acceptable option, had Nelson not faced another major obstacle: Lady Hamilton would not countenance the option of sailing home while Sir William, in poor health and low spirits, was convinced that the trip would kill him. Nelson decided that his only real option was to make the trip by land, even though this risked exposing them to attack by French land forces.

He put together a European wagon train, and set off for the long and staggered journey home. Their first call was at Florence, and then Ancona, where they were delayed for two weeks while waiting for a sea passage to Trieste and thence to Vienna. As they proceeded, the company found themselves hailed and applauded by happy mobs yelling, *"Viva Nelson!"*

By August they had arrived in Vienna, where they were introduced to Emperor Franz II and Empress Elisabeth, and where Nelson met some old friends, including Gilbert Eliot, Lord Minto. His wife, Lady Minto, reported:

> I don't think he has altered in the least. He has the same shock head and the same honest simple manners; but he is devoted to *Emma,* he thinks her quite an *angel,* and talks of her as such to her face and behind her back, and she leads him about like a keeper with a bear. She must sit by him at dinner to cut his meat, and he carries her pocket-handkerchief. He is a gig from ribbons, orders and stars, but he is just the same with us as he ever was.

Emma did not, on the whole, make a good impression. Though still beautiful, she was putting on weight (not surprising, when she ate so heartily and drank so deeply), was passionate about gambling, and generally struck her refined hosts as loud and vulgar. One gentleman reported that she almost never paused from laughing, singing, mimicking, and talking, while her lover remained quiet and withdrawn: "In a word, the Lord of the Nile seemed as clumsy and dim on land as he is adroit and notable at sea."

Nelson's party then went on to Prague, where Nelson was treated to a lavish celebratory banquet, and then to Dresden, where both Horatio and Emma were treated to portraits by the gifted court painter, Johann Heinrich Schmidt. It was also in Dresden that he was observed by a sharp-eyed, quizzical citizen, one Thomas Kosegarten. This man was struck by the contrast between Nelson's titanic reputation and his slight, damaged mortal frame. He thought Nelson

> ... one of the most insignificant-looking
> figures I ever saw in my life. His weight
> cannot be more than seventy pounds, and
> a more miserable collection of bones and
> wizened frame I have never yet come
> across. His bold nose, the steady eye and
> the solid worth revealed in his whole
> face betray in some measure the great
> conqueror. He speaks little, and then only
> English, and he hardly ever smiles. I have
> no doubt of his high ability, but one cannot
> look without astonishment at his slender
> body, although this can of course have no
> immediate connexion with his soul ...

The long journey home lasted until the start of November and included a visit to Hamburg, where a local pastor asked Nelson fervently to sign an antique Bible, as he considered him "the Saviour of the Christian World". The final stage of the journey was also the most unpleasant: a fierce storm blew up, and it took five days to reach their port of call in Great Yarmouth.

Nelson was immediately greeted by cheering crowds, and pressed in by people who wanted to thank and honour him. The landlady of a local pub, Sarah Suckling – she claimed to be a relative – asked if she could rename her hostel the Wrestler's Inn, calling it the "Nelson Arms" instead. In a rare flash of wit, Nelson replied: "That would be absurd, seeing that I have but one." There were services of thanksgiving, gun salutes, formal dinners, armed escorts, and yet more cheering crowds.

By 9 November, they reached London. It was here and now that Emma and Fanny, mistress and wife, finally met face to face. It went even worse than Nelson had feared. For Emma, it was hate at first sight, fed by envy as well as jealousy. Fanny was dignified, possessed of impeccable manners, and clearly much admired by Nelson's oldest friends and even his father. For her part, Fanny was dismayed by Emma's blowsy sensuality and her evident success – Emma was now pregnant – in having made Horatio her erotic slave.

For his part, Nelson made an attempt at decorous public display, and moved back home with Fanny for a few miserable months. He found her dignified ways chilly and uncomfortable, and repeatedly crept away from her to rejoin the Hamiltons. It was William Hamilton who joined Nelson at the City banquet in his honour, and Nelson chose to spend Christmas not with his wife but with the Hamiltons, who had been invited to stay at Fonthill, the lavish and eccentric creation of William Beckford. Thanks to the gleeful caricatures of Horatio, Fanny, William and Emma in the press, the whole nation was kept up to date with this glum comedy.

According to various tellings, this unpleasant marital conflict came to a head early in 1801, at the breakfast table. One version has it that conversation between Horatio and Fanny had been fairly cheerful until he tactlessly mentioned something that had been done by "dear Lady Hamilton". It was the last straw. Fanny rose from her chair and angrily declared that she was sick of hearing about "dear Lady Hamilton", and that Horatio must finally make up his mind between her and Emma.

He replied: "Take care, Fanny, what you say. I love you sincerely, but I cannot forget my obligations to Lady Hamilton, or speak of her otherwise than with affection and admiration." Fanny left the room, then the house, and the couple were never to live together again. Another, gentler version of this parting has them bidding sad but respectful, and even affectionate, farewell. What is beyond doubt is that the remainder of Fanny's life was starved of affection, though she was never known to rage against Nelson's defection. On the contrary, she became an increasingly sad and desolate soul.

Not that Nelson was in good spirits after the separation, either. His eye was troubling him badly, and he was confined to a dark room so as to give it rest. His dear friend William Locker died just after Christmas, and he was also made executor of the estate of his uncle William Suckling. Horatio's two early patrons had left him, and he was separated from Emma, to whom he wrote passionate notes every day.

On the positive side, he had a new mission; to the Baltic Sea. Britain had a new enemy, or more exactly enemies, to the north and east. Tsar Paul of Russia had decided to break his alliance with Britain and join the French. Accordingly, he had recruited other powers – Denmark, Sweden, and Prussia – to re-form an old alliance known as the "Armed Neutrality of the North". Now alone in the war against France, Britain was in urgent need of Scandinavian raw materials for shipbuilding and other essentials. The Admiralty decided to despatch a fleet to the Baltic Sea under the command of Admiral Sir Hyde Parker – not an inspired choice of leader, as he was elderly, recently married to a much younger woman, and given to caution. But their choice of the expedition's second-in-command could not be faulted: Nelson. He was given the *St George*: "… Lord Spencer says I must go forth as the Champion of England in the North."

On 30 January 1801, Emma gave birth to twin girls, one of whom died. The surviving daughter was christened Horatia. Nelson was ecstatic, but his joy was tempered by jealousy that bordered on obsession. He was convinced that the Prince of Wales, a notorious womaniser, would attempt to seduce Emma, and succeed.

On board the *St George*, he wrote his final known letter to Fanny. It strikes an unpleasant note of complacency:

> … I have done my duty as an honest,
> generous man, and I neither want or wish
> anybody to care what becomes of me,
> whether I return, or am left in the Baltic.
> Living, I have done all in my power for
> you, and if dead, you will find I have done
> the same; therefore my only wish is to be
> left to myself …

The Battle of Copenhagen (1801)

On 1 January, Nelson was promoted to Vice Admiral. Two weeks later, he took command of the HMS *San Josef.* With Fanny now out of his life for good, he could devote all his free time to dreaming of Emma. On 22 February, he wrote to Emma from Spithead, declaring that his yearning for her was so all-powerful as to render all other women uninviting: "… [W]ith my present feelings, I might be trusted with 50 virgins naked in a dark room."

On 12 March, he set sail, under the command of Parker, to the Baltic. On 2 April, the British fleet closed in on the Danes in what would soon become known as the Battle of Copenhagen.

The Danish ships were anchored close to shore, very much as the French fleet had been at Aboukir Bay. This time, though, it would not be possible to sail swiftly around them and attack from the rear, as the waters were too shallow. At first, the prospect of victory seemed remote, But, as Southey describes it:

> Nelson's agitation had been extreme when he saw himself, before the action began, deprived of a fourth part of his ships of the line. But no sooner was he in battle, where his squadron was received with the fire of more than a thousand guns, than, as if that artillery, like music, had driven away all care and painful thoughts, his countenance brightened; and, as a bystander describes him, his conversation became joyous, animated, elevated and delightful.

> … A shot through the mainmast knocked

the splinters about; and he observed to
one of his officers, with a smile: "It is
warm work; and this day may be the last
to any of us at a moment"; – and then
stopping short of the gangway, added, with
emotion – "But mark you: I would not be
elsewhere for thousands."

Then came one of the most celebrated incidents of
Nelson's career, which, slightly misremembered, has
passed into popular myth. Parker, unable to see clearly
for all the smoke raised by the battle, did note that some
British ships were in distress. Wishing to give Nelson the
opportunity to retreat if he judged it necessary, Parker had
his men hoist Signal No. 39: DISCONTINUE ACTION. The
lieutenant reported this to Nelson:

He continued his walk, and did not
appear to take notice of [the signal].
The lieutenant, meeting his Lordship at
the next turn, asked "whether he should
repeat it?" Lord Nelson answered, "No,
acknowledge it." On the officer returning
to the poop, his Lordship called after
him, "Is No.16, for close action, still
hoisted?" The lieutenant answering in
the affirmative, Lord Nelson said, "Mind
you keep it so." He now walked the deck
considerably agitated, which was always
known by his moving the stump of his right
arm. After a turn or two he said to me, in
a quick manner, "Do you know what's
shown on board of the Commander-in-

Chief? No. 39!" On asking him what that
meant he answered, "Why, to leave off
action." "Leave off action!", he repeated,
and then added, with a shrug, "Now damn
me if I do!" He also observed, I believe to
Captain Foley, "You know, Foley, I have
only one eye - I have a right to be blind
sometimes"; and then, with an archness
peculiar to his character, putting the glass
to his blind eye, he exclaimed: "I really do
not see the signal!"

In popular culture, this gesture is often remembered as
being accompanied by the words, "I see no ships!"

With the first blow solidly delivered, Nelson wrote a
brief letter that he sent ashore under a flag of truce.

TO THE BROTHERS OF
ENGLISHMEN, THE DANES.

Lord Nelson has orders to spare Denmark,
when no longer resisting; but if the firing
is continued on the part of Denmark, Lord
Nelson will be obliged to set on fire all the
Floating batteries he has taken, without
having the power to save the brave Danes
who have defended them. Dated on board
his Britannic Majesty's ship *Elephant*,
Copenhagen Roads, April 2nd 1801.

NELSON AND BRONTE, Vice-
Admiral, under the command of Admiral
Sir Hyde Parker.

Firing ceased.

The casualty list had been terrible: about 6,000 Danes were killed, wounded or taken prisoner. About 900 British soldiers and sailors met the same fate.

Nelson might well have expected a severe reprimand: once again (and not yet aware of Parker's intentions in giving the signal to retreat), he had apparently defied orders. As at Cape St Vincent, however, he was instead showered with praise for his brave initiative.

He was both ill and exhausted, yet Parker nonetheless sent him ashore to carry out tricky negotiations for peace with the Prince of Denmark, which he could quite easily and properly have done himself. Nelson and the prince spoke for just two hours, during which the admiral took pains to commend the valour of the Danish sailors: "The French fought bravely, but they could not have stood for one hour the fight which the Danes had supported for four."

Nelson succeeded as brilliantly with words as he had done with arms. Captain Hardy was astonished:
The more I see of his lordship, the more I admire his great character, for I think that on this occasion his Political Management was *if possible* greater than his bravery.

The general sense of triumph among the British was somewhat dampened when news reached them that, in retrospect, suggested that not only the negotiations but the battle itself had been unnecessary. On 24 March, a week before the hostilities, a group of dissident Russian officers had assassinated the tsar. The northern alliance against Britain – the "Armed Neutrality" – probably no longer existed, though as yet it was unclear what policy the new Tsar Alexander might pursue. Parker sailed to Sweden, where he encountered a Swedish squadron that tactfully retreated before battle could be joined. Despite this rather anti-climactic conclusion, Nelson remained exultant. He wrote to Emma:

> I received as a warrior all the praises which could gratify the ambitions of the vainest man and the thanks of the [Danish] nation ... for my humanity in saving the town from destruction. Nelson is warrior, but will not be a butcher.

Meanwhile, Parker had been ordered to test Russia's military intentions by confronting their ships at Rewa, in modern-day Poland. But Parker – cautious or cowardly, depending on his superiors' attitude – refused to carry out this order. He returned from Sweden to Copenhagen. The Lords of the Admiralty were furious with him, stripped him of his command and appointed Nelson in his place. On 6 May 1801, Nelson hoisted his flag as official Commander-in-Chief.

Tsar Alexander sent a blustering message that he could not negotiate a peace while British warships were still within easy striking distance of Russian ports. Nelson, once again excelling as a newly minted diplomat, sent an emollient reply that was perfectly judged so as not to wound Alexander's self-esteem. Just three days later, the Armed Neutrality was dissolved. The British action had been a success, and Nelson was awarded the credit. On 12 June, a despatch told him that he had been created a viscount; no less welcome news, he was now free to sail back to England.

On 1 July he landed at Yarmouth. His first move was to pay a visit to the naval hospital, the wards of which were crammed with the injured veterans of Copenhagen.

He also learned that his brother Maurice had just died of "brain fever". Of the eight sons of Catherine Nelson, only Horatio and William now survived. He was also pained by a letter from Fanny, an almost pitiable document that begged him to treat her with affection again:

I cannot be silent in the general joy throughout the kingdom. What my feelings are, your own good heart will tell you. Let me beg, nay, entreat you to believe no wife ever felt greater affection for a husband than I do, and, to the best of my knowledge, I have invariably done everything you desire. If I have omitted anything I am sorry for it ...

But Nelson made no reply.

Fanny had been right about one thing: Nelson had brought joy to the nation. The Admiralty was now proud of their man: a few weeks later, the First Lord, St Vincent, wrote to Nelson:

> I never saw a man in our Profession, excepting yourself and Troubridge, who possessed the magic art of infusing the same spirit into others, which inspired their own actions, exclusive of talents habits of business not common to Naval characters. Your Lordship's whole conduct, from your first appointment to this hour, is the subject of our constant admiration. It does not become me to make comparisons: all agree that there is but one Nelson.

Yet praise from such exalted quarters was most of the reward Nelson would receive for his Baltic feats. He bitterly resented the fact that there were others, including his king, who either slighted or simply ignored what he justly considered to be his military masterpiece. Lady Elizabeth Foster recorded an incident that wounded him deeply:

> "Lord Nelson", said George III, when
> the victor paid his respects after his return,
> "Do you get out?" And, said Nelson,
> "I was tempted to say: 'Sir, I have been
> out and am come in again. Your Majesty
> perhaps has not heard of the Battle of
> Copenhagen!'"

Merton and the Prelude to Trafalgar

On his return from the Baltic, Nelson was delighted to join the Hamiltons for some days of leisure in the English countryside – first at Box Hill, then in Staines, where Sir William enjoyed fishing in the Thames. But the idyll was short-lived; London was alive with rumours about an imminent French invasion. The Admiralty called Nelson back to active service, and made him Commander-in-Chief of an anti-invasion force.

On 27 July, he raised his flag on the captured French frigate *Unité*, then sailed down the coast to take over another frigate, the *Medusa*. On 1 August – the third anniversary of the Battle of the Nile – he sailed to Boulogne to recce the enemy positions. After some inconclusive attempts to harry the French, he sailed on from Flushing, but was driven by winds back to England.

After consultation with First Lord St Vincent, he decided to launch a major attack on Boulogne, with a force of fifty-seven boats in four divisions. Each would be manned by highly armed sailors, with orders to board enemy ships wielding cutlasses, pikes, and axes. But this time, Nelson had underestimated his adversary. Admiral Louis-René Levassor de Latouche-Tréville, predicting this strategy, had lined his twenty-four ships across the mouth of the harbour and fitted each with heavy nets; he also deployed several hundred soldiers. It would not be easy for the British.

The first setback came when the British ships, fighting strong currents, were dispersed so widely that no coordination was possible. Parker's division was the first to close with the French, and was met by a lethal burst of gunfire. Those who survived attempted to carry on with the planned attack, but were soon enmeshed in the giant defensive nets. The other three divisions also failed: one attempted an attack and was repulsed; another was swept back by the tides; and the last was driven so far away that it never went into action.

It was a terrible defeat, with a high death toll; proof that even Nelson was not infallible. He rented rooms in Deal, visited the wounded in the local hospital, mourned the dead, and yearned for Emma. He was also painfully aware that there were those who put the blame for the disaster wholly on him. There was even a strange blackmail attempt. A "Mr Hill" sent him a paper outlining what he saw as Nelson's misconduct in the Boulogne mission, and threatened that he would have his words published in a newspaper unless Nelson sent him a £100 banknote. He forwarded Hill's letter to the Admiralty, and to Hill himself wrote:

> Very likely I am unfit for my present
> command, and whenever Government
> change me, I hope they will find no

difficulty in selecting an Officer of greater
abilities; but you will, I trust, be punished
for threatening my character. But I have
not been brought up in the school of fear,
and therefore care not what you do. I defy
you and your malice.

He invited Sir William and Lady Hamilton to pay a visit
to Deal, and, finally, they came. He bloomed in their
presence, and when they left he was again plunged into
despair. He wrote to Emma in heartbroken terms, and
begged her to "prepare for me the farm" ...

The "farm" to which he referred was not, in fact, a
proper working one, but a large house in the London
suburb of Merton, about eight miles from Westminster.
Nelson bought it for the very considerable sum of £9,000,
which was more than he could afford without help.

On 1 October, an armistice was declared between Britain and France. A wave of enthusiasm and even joy spread
across the nation, but Nelson was not pleased. The French
had conceded withdrawal from Naples and the Papal
States, recognised the independence of the Ionian islands
and gave up their claim to Egypt. But Britain gave up far
more, surrendering almost all conquered territories (save
Ceylon [modern-day Sri Lanka] and Trinidad) to France,
Spain and Holland, and restoring Malta to the Knights of
St John. It was too much, Nelson thought, and anyone
who was pleased by the outcome was a fool.

Even so, he was determined to enjoy the pause in hostilities for as long as it might last. On 22 October, Nelson
made directly for Merton. The period of peace he enjoyed
there with the Hamiltons, which lasted until fresh hostilities
began in May 1803, were probably the happiest of his life.

For a short time, it seemed as if the future looked bright. France had made peace with the Holy Roman Empire in February 1802. In March, British ships destroyed the marooned French fleet in Aboukir Bay, where it had been stuck since Nelson's great victory. There were even talks of a treaty between France and Britain, which became a reality after Pitt resigned his office. The new administration, under Henry Addington, agreed to terms that, in effect, restored most of the territories captured by Britain. Nelson was horrified, and thought the agreement shameful. (It was certainly to prove fragile.) But for now, Nelson was free to go ashore and enjoy his life at Merton, as well as to play politics for a while. On 29 October, he took his seat in the House of Lords, and gave his maiden speech the following day. His first appearances were not impressive, but he rapidly gained confidence and flair.

Emma was thrilled by this development, and daydreamed of a bright future for Nelson as statesman and herself as his grand hostess. She was already presiding over many dinners at Merton. Not everyone was charmed by these feasts, nor by Emma. Lord Minto, for one, wrote to his wife:

> I went to Lord Nelson's on Saturday to dinner and returned today in the forenoon. The whole establishment and way of life is such as to make me angry as well as melancholy; but I cannot alter it and I do not think myself obliged or at liberty to quarrel with him for his weakness, though nothing shall ever induce me to give the smallest countenance to Lady Hamilton. She looks ultimately to the chance of

> marriage, as Sir W. will not be long in
> her way and she probably indulges a hope
> that she may survive Lady Nelson; in the
> meanwhile she and Sir William and the
> whole set of them are living with him at
> his expense. She is in high looks, but more
> immense than ever. She goes on cramming
> Nelson with trowel-fuls of flattery, which
> he goes on taking as quietly as a child does
> pap. The love she makes to him is not only
> ridiculous but disgusting ...

He went on to note, disdainfully, that the whole house had been made a temple to Nelson's glory, with paintings of the hero, coats of arms, crockery and gewgaws.

Nelson's health was still not good, and he made his indisposition the excuse for not attending his father's funeral in Norfolk. Edmund Nelson had died in Bath on 26 April 1802 and was buried at Burnham Thorpe. Horatio was indeed ill, but it seems likely that his main motive for this unfilial attitude was his dread of meeting Fanny again.

By this time, Nelson's unrivalled fame was given form in a torrent of prints, poems, pottery and assorted souvenirs. But amid all the idolatry there was now the increasingly frequent note of jeering at Nelson's private life. Representations of Emma bordered on the pornographic, while those of Hamilton showed him as a senile, impotent cuckold.

Yet for the vast majority Nelson was still the Hero, and such a hero as the nation had never seen. When, throughout July and August, he went on a long tour of Wales and the Midlands with the Hamiltons, the journey soon transformed into a kind of unofficial triumphal procession for Nelson, who was lionised and adored by the public wherever he went – Oxford, Blenheim, Gloucester, the Forest of Dean, Ross-on-Wye, Milford, Monmouth, Hereford, Birmingham, Warwick … each station of the journey was attended by cheering crowds, public ceremonies, theatrical celebrations, and feasts.

A well-known anecdote from this time was recalled some years later by the distinguished historical painter Benjamin West, who was famous for, among other portraits, *The Death of General Wolfe*. Nelson found himself seated next to West at a dinner, and the two men found much to admire in each other. Nelson, no doubt with the intention to flatter West in a dignified manner, said that one of his regrets was that he had never developed a taste for paintings, nor learned the arts of discrimination.

"But," Nelson went on, "there is one picture whose power I *do* feel. I never pass a print shop where your *Death of Wolfe* is in the window without being stopped by it." He asked West why he had done no more pictures in that vein.

"Because, my Lord," West replied, "there are no more subjects."

"Damn it! I didn't think of that," Nelson said, and urged West to take another glass of champagne.

"My Lord," the painter continued, "I fear that your intrepidity may yet furnish me with another such scene, and if it should, I shall certainly avail myself of it."

"Will you? *Will* you, Mr West? Then I hope I shall die in the next battle!"

A fine compliment, to be sure, but there is no reason to doubt that Nelson's sentiment was also quite sincere. He was to have his hope made real two years later.

By November 1802, Nelson was preparing to attend the House of Lords more frequently, at a time when war jitters had begun again. Abroad, Napoleon had been active again, and had annexed Piedmont; at home, there were wild rumours of insurrection. (One of these involved Nelson's comrade in Nicaragua many years before, Colonel Edward Despard. Nelson appeared as a character witness at Despard's trial, but to no effect: Despard was hanged on 21 Febuary 1803.)

There was other cause for despondency. On 8 April, the enfeebled Sir William Hamilton finally died. Emma held him in her arms during his final hours, while Nelson held his hand. With his customary regard for form, Nelson immediately moved away to another house, in Piccadilly, so as not to be seen as living under the same roof with the widow.

Little more than a month later, war with France began again. On 16 May, Nelson was appointed Commander-in-Chief of the Mediterranean. He hoisted his flag on the *Victory* at exactly the same hour on 18 May when France made a formal declaration of hostilities. Just as he sailed, he received the news that Emma was pregnant again.

The Victory

She was a very fine ship, built when Nelson was an infant and a child, and launched at Chatham in 1765. The captains who had commanded her included eminent mariners such as Viscount Keppel, Richard Kempenfelt, Howe, Hood and St Vincent. At the time Nelson hoisted his flag, she had just undergone an extensive set of repairs, so substantial as to amount to a virtual rebuild. Three decks high, she was a large floating fortress, yet remarkably swift.

Over 200 feet from stem to stern, her topmast rose to 175 feet above her deck. She had a 25-foot beam, a tonnage of over 200, and 104 guns. It took a crew of 850 men to work her, and to arrange the vast spread of sail that gave her power and speed. Nelson could not have hoped for a better flagship, nor for more comfortable and elegant personal quarters.

He had a large dining-cabin, sleeping quarters with adjoining rooms in which his team of personal assistants lived, including his steward Chevalier, who had pantries and a kitchen for the admiral's meals. His day-cabin, in which he read and wrote, was splendidly furnished with couches, various desks, portraits of Emma, and a silver bowl of fruit.

Nelson's initial orders were to rendezvous with his old friend Cornwallis, who was in the waters off Brest, offer *Victory* as a reinforcement, and, should Cornwallis declare that he needed no extra force (as was expected), to proceed into the Mediterranean. On 6 July, *Victory* joined the Navy off Toulon; Nelson's orders were "to take, sink, burn or otherwise destroy" all the French ships anchored there.

They sailed past Lisbon, stopped for a day at Gibraltar, and then sailed to Naples by way of Malta. The sight of Naples stirred Nelson, though, now under the *de facto* control of France, it was no longer the city of his erotic awakening. By 8 July, *Victory* joined the British squadron blockading Toulon. Nelson learned that the French naval commander at Toulon was none other than Admiral Latouche-Tréville, who had been in charge of the force that had repelled him at Boulogne two years earlier.

The blockade was hard for the British: their ships were battered and damaged, their men beginning to fall victim to scurvy. Nelson himself was in a bad way: "I really believe that my shatter'd carcase is in the worst plight of the whole fleet." He was suffering from rheumatic fever, night sweats, violent spasms, and pains in his heart and side. The political and military news was also grim. Napoleon had declared himself Emperor, and persuaded Spain to join in war against Britain again.

The year 1805 began badly. On 1 January, the French squadron at Rochefort managed to slip through the British line. Two weeks later, Admiral Villeneuve had led a French force out of Toulon under cover of dark and sailed off, destination unknown. Malta? Naples? Egypt? Nelson at once set off on a search for them with a party of eleven sails of the line and two frigates. But the search was fruitless, and lasted until, in Malta, Nelson heard the anti-climactic news that in fact Villeneuve's force had been driven back to Toulon by storms.

Napoleon had devised a plan to thwart Nelson. He gave Admiral Villeneuve the order to escape Toulon a second time, and then to lure Nelson's force away from the Mediterranean on a wild goose chase to the West Indies. When Nelson received a report that Villeneuve had sailed past Gibraltar and headed west, he took the bait and set off in pursuit – but he never caught sight of the enemy.

When Nelson's fleet reached Barbados, he was told that the French had already sailed south towards Trinidad. He proceeded to Grenada, then the Leeward Islands – both of which had been attacked – and Antigua. Eventually, reality dawned on him: the French had already left, and were on their way back to Europe. He set sail for Gibraltar, and anchored there on 20 July.

Downhearted, he applied to the Admiralty for a long-overdue leave, which was granted. In August he made his final trip to England, staying in Merton. Somewhat to his surprise, his failure – as he saw it – in the West Indian hunt had only added to his fame ad popularity. The Hero had chased the enemy halfway around the world!

Shortly before returning to the *Victory*, Nelson had an

encounter that has fascinated posterity. Sometime around 11 to 13 September, he met a soldier eleven years younger but already trailing a string of military triumphs unrivalled since the days of Marlborough: this was Sir Arthur Wellesley, later to be made Duke of Wellington. This was the one and only meeting between the victor of Trafalgar and the victor of Waterloo. Many years after the event, Wellington told a friend that "Lord Nelson was, in different circumstances, two quite different men", adding:

> I only saw him once in my life, and for, perhaps, an hour. It was soon after I returned from India. I went to the Colonial Office in Downing Street, and there I was shown into the little waiting room on the right hand, where I found also waiting to see the Secretary of State, a gentleman whom from his likeness to his pictures and the loss of an arm, I immediately recognized as Lord Nelson. He could not know who I was, but he entered at once into conversation with me, if I can call it conversation, for it was almost all on his side and all about himself, and in really, a style so vain and so silly as to surprise and almost disgust me.

I suppose that something that I happened to say may have made him guess that I was *somebody*, and he went out of the room for a moment, I have no doubt to ask the office-keeper who I was, for when he came back he was altogether a different man, both in manner and matter. All that I had thought a charlatan style had vanished, and he talked of the state of the country and of the aspect and probabilities of affairs on the Continent with a good sense, and a knowledge of subjects both at home and abroad, that surprised me equally and more agreeably than the first part of the interview had done; in fact, he talked like an officer and a statesman.

The Secretary of State kept us long waiting, and certainly, for the last half or three-quarters of an hour, I don't know that I ever had a conversation that interested me more. Now, if the Secretary of State had been punctual, and admitted Lord Nelson in the first quarter of an hour, I should have had the same impression of a light and trivial character that other people have had, but luckily I saw enough to be satisfied that he was really a very superior man; but certainly a more sudden and complete metamorphosis I never saw.

While ashore, Nelson thought carefully through his plan of attack on the enemy, and outlined it both to his naval colleagues and to Prime Minister Addington. It was a daring, perhaps even foolhardy plan that went against the fundamental philosophy of tactics that had dominated the Navy throughout the eighteenth century.

Briefly put, his strategy would be to "break the line". He would divide his fleet into three divisions. One, made up of the fastest ships, would be held in reserve while the other two, with the heavy guns, would go for the enemy at right angles, smash through and break the line at two places, thus dividing them into three. It was a plan almost without precedent in the previous 200 years.

On 2 September, a messenger brought despatches, which informed him that Villeneuve had joined with a force from La Coruña, and had taken refuge in the port of Cádiz. He had more than thirty French and Spanish ships of the line. Cádiz was the target. Nelson was annoyed by the suggestion from some politicians that he should merely enforce another blockade: "It is, as Mr Pitt knows, annihilation that the country wants ..."

On 14 September, Nelson boarded the *Victory* at Portsmouth. She sailed the following day. On 28 September, he took command of the fleet off Cádiz.

His arrival electrified the men. Seventeen thousand of them rejoiced, cheered, and wept. It was, Nelson wrote to a naval colleague, "the sweetest sensation in my life". Now the task was to wait for the enemy to come out from its lair and to engage it. Nelson filled the anxious interval by writing letters to Emma, and reading those she sent by return.

At last, on 18 October, there came signals that the enemy was finally starting to come out of port. By 20 October they were all at sea, though it was still not clear what Villeneuve intended. In fact, Napoleon had ordered Villeneuve to land troops at Naples and then make for Toulon. The movement of his ships was closely observed. Nelson, not wanting to scare Villeneuve back into port, set a parallel course, about 20 miles to the west. Finally, at 4 AM on the 21st, Nelson ordered a change of course to the north-east – directly towards the combined fleet.

Over the coming hours, Nelson would fight the most decisive sea battle in the history of the Western world.

Chapter Six

Trafalgar and Afterwards

The Battle of Trafalgar, 21 October
It was Collingwood's ship, the *Royal Sovereign*, that first closed with the enemy. Sailing well ahead of the main squadron, he broke the line astern of the Spanish vessel *Santa Ana*. Collingwood fought for about twenty minutes without reinforcements; his ship had the most powerful, deadly gunnery in the British fleet. "See how that noble fellow Collingwood takes his ship into action!" Nelson said. "How I envy him!" Collingwood, knowing his friend well, guessed these sentiments: "What would Nelson give to be here!"

Battle was fairly joined, and the *Victory* came under fire just a few minutes later. The first shot fell short; the second went into the sea alongside; and the third flew harmlessly over. Nelson ordered his frigate captains back to their various ships, with orders that each British vessel should adopt whichever tactic seemed most likely to bring them alongside enemy ships. As the captain of the *Eury-*

alus, Henry Blackwood, climbed over the side, Nelson made an uncharacteristically fatalist remark: "God bless you, Blackwood. I shall never speak to you again ..."

The firing grew heavier. One shot across the quarterdeck hit John Scott, Nelson's secretary, and tore him almost in half. An officer ordered his body thrown overboard at once. Nelson noticed: "Is that poor Scott?"

Because *Victory* was sailing directly towards the enemy line, its side-mounted guns could not be used. For the duration, she had no choice but to endure heavy raking fire from stem to stern. Further shots smashed the ship's wheel, destroying it, so the *Victory* had to be steered by a team of forty men pulling on the tiller. Another blast killed many of the marines who had been lined up to engage enemy snipers. Nelson ordered the survivors to disperse about the deck.

Meanwhile, he and Captain Hardy walked up and down, ostentatiously calm under heavy fire. One shot missed them so narrowly that it tore off the buckle of Hardy's shoe. "This is too warm work to last long," Nelson reassured him.

The crew kept their nerve, much to Nelson's delight, waiting for the manoeuvre that would finally allow them to return fire. Finally, at about half past twelve, Nelson gave the decisive order: the *Victory* ported to helm and let loose its formidable firepower. Their first target was Villeneuve's *Bucentaure*. Fifty heavy guns blasted away at the ship, smashing in her stern, destroying some twenty guns and, soon, killing half her crew. But then the *Neptune*, an eighty-four gunner, came in to attempt a rescue, and raked *Victory* with further broadsides.

It was a hell of smoke, flame and explosions. There were two other enemy ships at hand: the huge Spanish four-decker *Santísima Trinidad* and the French *Redoutable*, which now raked the *Victory* so fiercely as to almost clear the decks. Their orders were to capture or sink Nelson's ship, and they might have succeeded had not the *HMS Temeraire* sailed in to defend her.

The crew of the *Victory* retaliated by throwing more than 200 grenades aboard the *Redoutable*, but despite this deadly barrage, a few French sailors managed briefly to board the *Victory*. Before they could press their advantage, the *Temeraire* came up on the starboard and fired on the French ship so severely that she sank the next day. The *Redoutable* suffered the worst damages of any vessel in the battle, with almost 500 killed and eighty wounded.

An official history of the battle commended Nelson for courage that surprised even his admirers:

> Oft did the little man himself, with his
> remaining eye, cast an anxious glance
> towards the Franco-Spanish line in search
> of the ship he meant the *Victory* first to
> grapple with, and so lightly did Lord
> Nelson value personal risk, that although
> urged more than once on the subject,
> he would not suffer those barriers from
> the Enemy's grape and musketry, the
> hammocks, to be placed one inch higher
> than, to facilitate his view of objects around
> him, they were accustomed to being placed.

It was, perhaps, an *excessive* bravery. At about a quarter past one, Hardy saw the admiral fall to his knees, supporting himself with his left arm; then his arm failed, and he collapsed. A sniper had singled him out and shot him.

"They have done for me at last, Hardy."

"I hope not."

"Yes. My backbone is shot through."

A marine and two sailors lifted Nelson and, on Hardy's orders, carried him down the ladders to the surgeon's station below. As they carried him, Nelson took out a handkerchief and covered his face with it, so that the men should not know their admiral had been wounded. The surgeon, William Beatty, was already busy with more than forty gravely wounded sailors. When Nelson saw Beatty's face, he said: "Ah, Mr Beatty! You can do nothing for me. I have but a short time to live; my back is shot through." His self-diagnosis was correct, and Beatty knew it. Still, the surgeon ordered Nelson carefully stripped of his blood-soaked clothes – tainted fabrics were a common cause of infection – and tried to examine the wound.

Beatty discovered that a ball had struck the left shoulder, penetrated downward into the chest, and (he guessed) lodged in the spine. Beatty asked Nelson to describe his symptoms: Nelson said that he had no feeling in the lower part of his body, but that he had felt the ball break his back. He also complained of a repeated gush of blood within his chest, and said that he was hot and thirsty, They brought him lemonade and watered wine, and cooled him with a fan. For a while, all he could say was "Fan, fan … drink, drink …"

In the seas around them, the battle raged as Nelson had planned: "pell-mell". At one point a cheer went up from the deck above – evidently an enemy ship had struck her colours. Nelson thirsted for news as well as fluids, and asked that Hardy be sent to him as quickly as possible; he was told that Hardy was fully engaged on deck, but would be down as soon as he could.

Villeneuve's ship had been battered to a near-wreck by *Victory's* guns, and then by the *Conqueror*; soon, all her masts had been smashed, and Villeneuve surrendered to the *Conqueror* at about a quarter past two. By now, every British ship had singled out its enemy counterpart, and the battle had become a series of duel-like actions, with both sides firing dreadful volleys at each other from close range. The smoke was so thick that sometimes the ships lost sight of their immediate opponent; but it soon became clear that the British were winning their duels.

At about half past two, Hardy finally had time to confer with Nelson. His news of the fight was as cheering as Nelson's of his ebbing vitality was grim. Hardy began:

"We have got twelve or fourteen of the enemy's ships in our possession. But five of theirs have tacked and show an intention of bearing down on the *Victory*. I have therefore called two or three of our fresh ships around us and I have no doubt of giving them a drubbing."

"I hope none of our ships have struck?"

"No, my Lord. There is no fear of that."

A pause. Then Nelson said: "I am a dead man, Hardy. I am going fast. It will all be over with me soon. Come nearer to me. Pray let my Lady Hamilton have my hair and all the other things belonging to me."

"Is your pain great?"

"Yes, but I shall live half an hour longer yet."

Hardy went back up to his tasks on deck, and Beatty returned to his patient. Nelson told him that he had now lost all sensation beneath his upper chest and knew that he was a hopeless case. Beatty wept, and turned away to hide his tears. "God be praised, I have done my duty," said Nelson, and repeated the phrase several times over the following minutes.

About an hour later, Hardy came back, took Nelson by the hand, and congratulated him upon a brilliant victory. He was not entirely sure how many ships had been taken, but it must be at least fifteen, and the enemy had surrendered.

"That is well," Nelson said, and – perfectionist to the last – "but I had bargained for twenty." He gave Hardy the order for the whole fleet to anchor once the fighting was completely done, because he remembered that a terrible gale that was brewing, and must surely hit them in a just a few hours, if not before.

Then came the most famous moment of his dying hour.

"Do not throw me overboard, Hardy!"

"Oh, no, certainly not!"

"Then you know what to do. Take care of my dear Lady Hamilton, Hardy, take care of poor Lady Hamilton." Then, faintly: "Kiss me, Hardy."

(There is no evidence at all for the suggestion, sometimes put forth, that what Nelson had, in fact, said was, "Kismet, Hardy.") His friend understood him, and kissed Nelson's cheek.

"Now I am satisfied. Thank God I have done my duty."

Hardy stood, and then knelt down again to kiss Nelson's brow. By this time, the admiral's sight was fading,

"Who is that?"

"It is Hardy."

"God bless you, Hardy."

Nelson's breathing became slow and shallow. To the attending chaplain, he whispered: "Doctor, I have not been a *great* sinner." He spoke again of Lady Hamilton and Horatia, kept thanking God he had done his duty, urged them to rub his chest to ease the pain, and then lost the power of speech.

At half past four, Beatty pronounced him dead.

Shortly afterwards, Beatty carried out a thorough post-mortem. It revealed that, in spite of Nelson's many wounds, his brain, lungs, kidneys, and most other organs were all in good condition, more typical of a man in his late twenties than his late forties. Had the sniper missed, Nelson could easily have lived a long and active life – perhaps as a politician, as his ambitions in that direction had been growing in his final years; perhaps even as Prime Minister.

But even as the danger of battle was over, the dangers of the elements began. The huge gale that Nelson had feared now hit victors and losers alike indiscriminately, throwing their ships around violently, and adding to the miseries of the exhausted and wounded combatants. Its force was so terrible that only four of the seventeen captured enemy ships survived, and it would be several days before the scale of the victory could be judged. British losses were heavy: 1,700 dead or seriously injured, though not a single ship had been taken. Enemy losses were far greater: 6,000 men killed or wounded, 20,000 (including Villeneuve) taken prisoner. If not quite the complete annihilation Nelson had planned, it was nevertheless overwhelming.

Jubilation was all but drowned in sorrow for the lost leader. The young boatswain's mate was unable to pipe the hands to quarters because he was sobbing: "Hang me, I can't do it! To lose him now! I wouldn't have cared if it had been my old father, brother, or sisters if there were fifty more of them – but I can't think of parting with Nelson!"

As popular tradition recalls, and for once correctly, Nelson's remains were preserved in a cask of brandy – changed, after the fleet had docked at Gibraltar for repairs and urgent medical treatment, to spirits of wine – and was lashed to the mainmast with a guard mounted around the clock.

News of Nelson's death spread rapidly across the Mediterranean. One of the first English civilians to learn his fate was the poet Samuel Taylor Coleridge, who was at that time in Naples, slowly making his way back to England after completing his period of civil service in Malta with Sir Alexander Bell. Coleridge wrote:

> When word of Nelson's death at last
> reached England on 6 November, he had
> been dead for seventeen days. Rightly, one
> of the first to be brought the sorry news
> was Emma. The Admiralty had despatched
> a meek, softly spoken man, Mr Whitby,
> as their messenger. Emma ordered her
> servants to have him brought in directly.
> He began, nervously:
> "We have gained a great victory..."
> "Never mind your victory - my letters,
> give me my letters!", she interrupted him,
> meaning love letters from her Horatio.
> Whitby could not bring himself to speak
> any more. He wept in silence. Emma gave a
> scream, and collapsed. She was incapable of
> speech or movement for the next ten days.

Elsewhere – and this is richly documented fact, not mere propaganda – the British were plunged into a state of mourning and shock. Not until the funeral of Sir Winston Churchill, or, to take a more recent example, that of Princess Diana, was the nation so convulsed with grief. Their greatest hero had gone – had died in the very act of saving them from the monster Napoleon.

From 4 – 7 January 1806, Nelson's corpse was allowed to lie in state in the Painted Hall of the Royal Hospital in

Greenwich. More than 15,000 people came to pay their respects: so many that the authorities feared a macabre kind of riot, and ordered sailors to turn their pikes on the crowd. As he had long intended, Nelson was interred in the coffin made from the wood of the *Orient* (destroyed in his great victory at the Battle of the Nile), gifted to him by Admiral Hallowell.

On 8 January the coffin was placed on a barge, which sailed slowly westwards up the Thames. It was then deposited at the Admiralty in Whitehall. That night was bitterly cold, and few Londoners could manage to sleep. Parties had been arriving from all over England in the previous few days, and all the inns and hostels were crammed with guests. Some did not even attempt to sleep, but walked the streets in search of the best vantage points along the funeral route.

Finally, the sun came up, and after days of overcast weather, drizzle and fog, it was dazzling. By 8.30 AM, the bells of St Paul's began to toll. Nearly every mourner was now either seated by the roadside or leaning out from an upper window. The funeral procession, its centrepiece a hearse modelled on the *HMS Victory* – included more than 10,000 troops led by the Royal Scots Greys cavalry regiment. It reached the cathedral well before the senior officers bringing up the rear had even left the Admiralty. Later, everyone remarked on a strange noise that had filled the air. Though the crowds had maintained a respectful silence, the effect of thousands of people doffing their hats in unison sounded, aptly, like the murmurings of the sea.

By the time the congregation had finally gathered inside St Paul's, daylight was waning, and for a while, all was gloom. But then a new chandelier made up of 130 lamps was illuminated, and cast its brilliance over the service. In all, the ceremony lasted about four hours. At the end of it, Nelson's coffin was lowered into the crypt, where it was interred in a large marble sarcophagus, commissioned in the sixteenth century by Cardinal Wolsey, before his fall from royal favour. Villeneuve, a prisoner of war, was among the mourners; how strange this touch of chivalry now seems. Sadly, the same chivalrous spirit did not extend to Lady Hamilton, who was pointedly not invited; Lady Nelson was the official widow. Nor, shamefully, did the government ever grant Emma the pension and other favours for which the hero had begged. Her remaining few years were pitiful. She rapidly overspent herself into debt, drank heavily and ended her days as an almost unknown pauper in Calais, where she died from alcoholic excess and the illnesses of poverty.

The last part of the funeral was unplanned and unexpected. Surviving members of the *Victory* were meant to furl three of their ship's flags – riddled with bullet-holes – and lay them upon the coffin. Instead, the men fell upon the largest flag, tore a great strip from it and divided it between them, so that each man should have a proper relic of their fallen leader. No one who watched this rending saw it as anything than a sincere gesture of love.

It was the grandest funeral of any English man of war since that of the poet and soldier Sir Philip Sidney under Elizabeth I. Had Nelson truly deserved it? None of his contemporaries had any doubt. Here was the man who had saved them from invasion by Napoleon, and so from perpetual tyranny. This ideal view of Nelson prevailed throughout the nineteenth century and well into the early twentieth. As the saviour of his nation, he was revered only a little less than the Saviour of the World.

Even today, when the heroes of the British Empire are regarded with greater coolness and suspicion, Nelson remains a figure of world-historical stature. Whatever misgivings the twenty-first century has about certain aspects of his character and career, few have ever doubted his genius as a master of naval tactics, his almost unparalleled capacity to inspire the admiration and even love of his men, his personal courage, and his unswerving devotion to his duty as he saw it.

His fellow countrymen were right: Nelson's overwhelming victory had indeed, as they believed, put paid for good to Napoleon's plans to invade England – a threat as serious in its day as the prospect of a Nazi invasion in 1940. Trafalgar more or less thwarted all French ambitions at sea, and made possible the European land wars that culminated ten years later with Napoleon's final defeat at Waterloo. Nelson established Britain's supremacy on the seas, which in effect meant supremacy around the globe. This hegemony lasted for more than a century, during which Britain was the most powerful nation in the world. Very few of the battles waged since the days of the Roman Empire have shaped Western history so profoundly. Nelson was Britain's artist of war, and Trafalgar was his masterpiece.

Mayflower: The Voyage from Hell

Kevin Jackson looks at the reality behind the mythic status of the Mayflower – and the journey that 'created' the New World. Most of the voyagers of that famed 1620 crossing of the Atlantic were not in fact religious pilgrims, but people intent on forging a better life for themselves in the virgin territory of America's east coast. 130 hardy souls were confined in a space no bigger than a tennis court, braving the 'Northern' crossing, without any firm idea of what awaited them in the New World. A riveting account of the sailing that changed the world.

The Queen's Pirate: Sir Francis Drake & the Golden Hind

The Queen's Pirate: Sir Francis Drake & the Golden Hind tells the extraordinary story of Drake's early years and his journey around the world on his famous ship, the Golden Hind. For more than four centuries, Drake has been world-famous for his feats as a master mariner – the captain who "singed the King of Spain's beard" with his daredevil attack on the fleet at Cadiz, and who led the British Navy to victory against the Spanish Armada in 1588. But Drake's exploits in his earlier years, though less well known, are even more remarkable. Born into a poor, obscure family, he worked his way rapidly up in the maritime world to his first captaincy. Before long, he was the most successful of all English pirates, admired by his countrymen, hated and feared by the Spanish. Queen Elizabeth saw the potential in this rough-mannered but enterprising young man, and gave him her blessing for the first British venture into the Pacific Ocean. This success of this voyage, which lasted for three years, exceeded their wildest hopes. Not only did Drake come home with a vast treasure of captured gold, silver and jewels; he became the first man ever to circumnavigate the globe in a single mission, and bring most of his crew home alive and well.

Also launching soon in the *Seven Ships Maritime History* series: Nelson's *Victory*, Cooke's *Endeavour*, Shackleton's *Endurance* and Bligh's *Bounty*. All available directly, including signed copies, from the publisher at: www.canofworms.net